MICRO
MONSTERS

MICRO
MONSTERS

Tom Jackson

Sandy Creek

Editorial and design by
Amber Books Ltd

Project Editor: Sarah Uttridge
Picture Research: Terry Forshaw
Designer: Zoe Mellors

ISBN- 978-1-4351-2655-8

Printed and bound in China

Manufactured July 2010

Lot 10 9 8 7 6 5 4 3 2 1

Picture Credits:
Special thanks to **Science Photo Library** for supplying all of the images in this book. Individual photographers and agencies are
credited below.
Scott Bauer: 57; John Bavosi: 131; Juergen Berger: 50; George Bernard: 67; Thierry Berrod, Mona Lisa Production: 12, 36; Adrian
Bicker: 75; Simon Booth: 151; Dr. John Brackenbury: 15, 19, 99; Dr. Tony Brain: 28, 176; Dr. Jeremy Burgess: 79; Scott
Camazine: 71, 81; Nigel Cattlin: 89, 105, 111; Jack Clark/Agstockusa: 49, 107; Crown Copyright Fera: 43; Andy Crump, TDR,
WHO: 177; Thomas Deerinck, NCMIR: 20, 62; Michael Delarme: 158; Georgette Doawma: 143; Martin Dohrn: 85, 125; Robert
Dunne: 145; Eye of Science: 23, 26, 64, 80, 108, 109, 116, 117, 128, 129, 130, 132, 134, 162, 174, 175, 180, 186, 187; M.T.
Frazier: 147; Bob Gibbons: 91; Pascal Goetgheluck: 37, 46, 47, 65; Eric Grave: 135; Russell Graves: 133; E. Gray: 137; Steve
Gschmeissner: 6, 10, 13, 30, 31, 33, 34, 40, 58, 70, 72, 74, 87, 92, 94, 96, 98, 100, 102, 104, 112, 114, 122, 124, 136, 146, 150,
152, 155, 156, 160, 172; Gusto Images: 17, 61, 93; Andy Harmer: 149; Jan Hinsch: 140; James King-Holmes: 154; Ted Kinsman:
45; Stephen J. Krasemann: 35; Christian Laforsch: 148; George D. Lepp: 141; Lucent Technologies Bell Labs: 144; Dr. P. Marazzi:
119, 121; Fred McConnaughey: 169; Tom McHugh: 183; Astrid & Hanns-Frieder Michler: 27; Susumu Nishinaga: 78, 82, 84, 90,
184; Claude Nuridsany & Marie Perennou: 21, 68, 88; Photostock Israel: 69; Simon D. Pollard: 83; Power & Syred: 8, 18, 22, 24,
38, 39, 51, 60, 76, 161; Dr. Morley Read: 25, 59, 73, 165; J.C.Revy: 106; James H. Robinson: 182; Chris Sattleberger: 153;
Francoise Sauze: 101; David Scharf: 48, 118, 120, 127, 164, 166, 188; Science Pictures Ltd: 16, 86; Gregory K. Scott: 103;
Alexander Semenov: 138, 142, 157; Sinclair Stammers: 11, 29, 115, 167, 181, 185, 189; Volker Steger: 14, 32, 42, 44, 52, 53, 54,
56, 66, 110, 123, 126, 168, 170, 171, 178, 179; Steve Taylor: 55; Kenneth H. Thomas: 97; Gianni Tortoli: 173; Dr. Keith
Wheeler: 159; Jeanne White: 77; Stuart Wilson: 95

Contents

Introduction	6		
AT HOME	8		
Bedbug	10		
Carpet Beetle	12		
Clothes Moth	14		
Cockroach	16		
Crane fly	18		
Daddy Long-Legs Spider	20		
Dust Mite	22		
Earwig	24		
Housefly	26		
House Spider	28		
Mange Mite	30		
Silverfish	32		
Spider's Web	34		
Wood Termite	36		
Woodworm	38		
FOOD BUGS	40		
Colorado Potato Beetle	42		
Blowfly	44		
Cheese Mite	46		
Fruit Fly	48		
Grain Weevil	50		
Ham Beetle	52		

Maggot	54
Meal Moth	56
Mealybug	58
Rosemary Beetle	60
IN THE BACKYARD	62
Ant	64
Aphid	66
Butterfly	68
Centipede	70
Cicada	72
Dung Fly	74
Earthworm	76
Honeybee	78
Hornet	80
Hoverfly	82
Jumping Spider	84
Lacewing	86
Ladybug	88
Long Horned Beetle	90
Millipede	92
Paper Wasp	94
Parasitic Wasp	96
Scale Insect	98
Slug	100
Springtail	102

Stinkbug	104
Thrips	106
Velvet Mite	108
ON THE BODY	112
Biting Midge	114
Eyelash Mite	116
Head Louse	118
Hookworm	120
Human Flea	122
Leech	124
Liver Fluke	126
Sand Flea	128
Scabies Mite	130
Stable Fly	132
Tapeworm	134
Threadworm	136
UNDER WATER	138
Brine Shrimp	140
Bristleworm	142
Brittle Star	144
Caddisfly	146
Dragonfly	148
Great Diving Beetle	150
Jellyfish	152

Pond Snail	154
Ragworm	156
Sea Urchin	158
Water Bear	160
IN THE DANGER ZONE	162
Assassin Bug	164
Blackfly	166
Cone Shell	168
Fire-Detecting Beetle	170
Locust	172
Lyme Disease Tick	174
Malaria Mosquito	176
Paralysis Tick	178
Sandfly	180
Tarantula	182
Tiger Mosquito	184
Tsetse Fly	186
Yellow-Fever Mosquito	188
Glossary	190
Index	191

Introduction

SO YOU THINK HUMAN BEINGS RULE THE WORLD? Well, think again. There may be six billion of us—and counting—but that is nothing compared to the trillions upon trillions of micromonsters that live all around us. There are countless more insects, spiders, worms, and other squirmy creatures running, wriggling, and flying all over our planet. But we are much bigger than them, right? Kind of: The weight of the human race is about 100 million tons. The weight of just the world's ants alone is at least 10 times that. And that is not counting the millipedes, midges, mites, and millions of other types of micromonster that overrun the Earth. Feeling small? Perhaps it's time you got to know a few. You may be aware of some of them from time to time, such as a housefly or wasp buzzing past, but have you ever taken a really good look?

With the naked eye, you cannot really see much, maybe some legs and shiny eyes. The problem is getting the minibeasts to stay still long enough to get a good look. Microscopes are like telescopes in reverse. Instead of making things far away look nearer, they make small things seem bigger so you can get a better look at them. Looking in bright light, the tiny creatures take on a more complicated shape. But to get a closer look still you need to turn off the lights—and use a beam of electrons. Electron microscopes can take you eye-to-eye with the micromonsters. They may look like terrifying creatures from a sci-fi movie but they are very real. One is probably watching you right now…

At Home

HOME IS WHERE THE HEART IS, they say. Well, home is also where the maggots, dust mites, and killer spiders are, too. Insects, spiders, and other types of micromonster have been living in people's homes every since we've lived in them. The minibeasts like the same things about our homes as we do: They are warm and dry and there is normally plenty of food.

A human home is not such an unnatural place when you look at it. Most of the things we use to make a place comfortable to live are natural products. Wool, cotton, wood, and leather all started out in the wild at some point. And now these things have become household objects, they have brought the insects and other critters that live on them along, too.

The home-loving micromonsters are just as happy living in a deep carpet or in a crack under the floorboards as they would be in the wild. To them there is no difference between the wood in some antique furniture as the dead logs in a woodland, or the rotting food in the garbage can and the corpse of an animal decaying in a ditch.
It is time to explore the hidden microworld of your home: Prepare to be shocked, scared, and just a little bit sickened.

Bedbug

Cimicidae

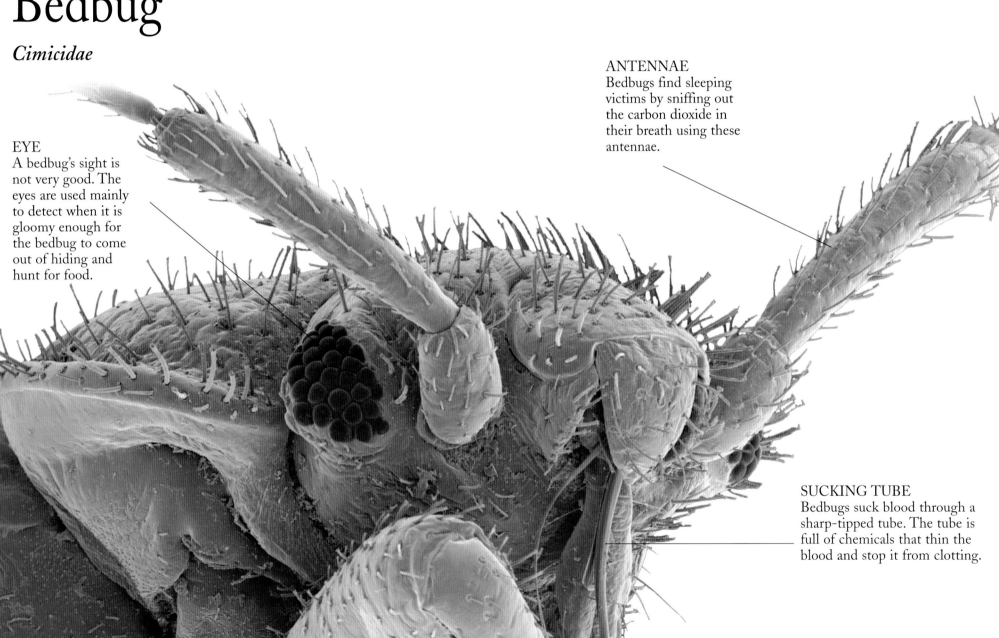

ANTENNAE
Bedbugs find sleeping victims by sniffing out the carbon dioxide in their breath using these antennae.

EYE
A bedbug's sight is not very good. The eyes are used mainly to detect when it is gloomy enough for the bedbug to come out of hiding and hunt for food.

SUCKING TUBE
Bedbugs suck blood through a sharp-tipped tube. The tube is full of chemicals that thin the blood and stop it from clotting.

edbugs are tiny bloodsuckers that come out only at night. They are looking for a sleeping animal—and a person in bed is just what they need. They take just a few minutes to eat their fill and can swallow five times their own body weight in blood in one meal. The bugs are just ⅛in (3mm) long and hide among the bedclothes or cracks in the furniture. It is hard to spot a single bedbug, but where there is one, there will probably be hundreds more nearby. A room with a bedbug problem may have a sweet smell from the bugs' watery waste. Getting rid of the all bugs will take a lot of careful cleaning.

Full point
(Magnified 5 times)

Bedbug
(Magnified 5 times)

SIZE COMPARISON

▶ BEDBUGS HAVE FLATTENED bodies so they can squeeze into the narrowest of hiding places. Once it has eaten a meal of blood, the bug will find a place to rest and will not need to eat again for several days.

Cave Creatures

Bedbugs have been around for millions of years—long before beds were invented. Experts think these little insects were once cave creatures that fed on the blood of bats and birds. Then early humans set up home in the caves, too, and bedbugs have been biting us ever since.

Did you know?

• In Bulgaria, people used to defend their beds from bugs by hanging runner-bean leaves around the edges. They thought the bedbugs would be trapped in the leaves' thick hairs.

• Bedbugs are less of a problem today—as long as you keep your bedclothes clean.

• Bedbugs do not spread diseases like some biting insects, but they can cause an itchy rash.

Carpet Beetle

Dermestidae

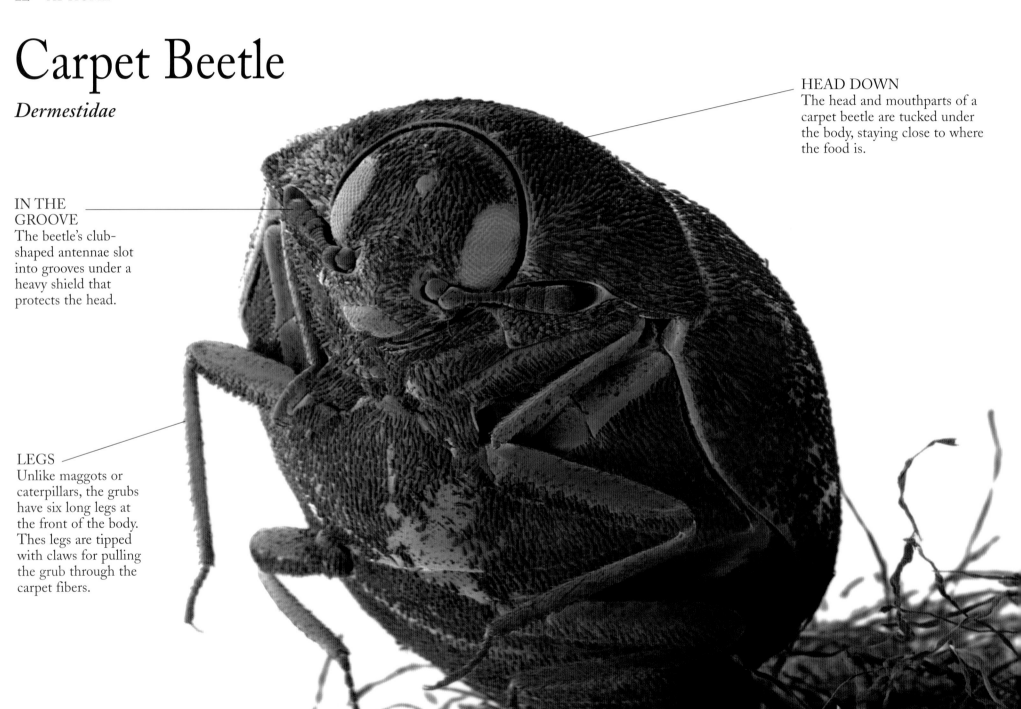

HEAD DOWN
The head and mouthparts of a carpet beetle are tucked under the body, staying close to where the food is.

IN THE GROOVE
The beetle's club-shaped antennae slot into grooves under a heavy shield that protects the head.

LEGS
Unlike maggots or caterpillars, the grubs have six long legs at the front of the body. Thes legs are tipped with claws for pulling the grub through the carpet fibers.

Millions of years ago, carpet beetles lived at the bottom of a bird's nest or on the floor of an animal's den. Their grubs survived by eating the hairs, feathers, and bits of dead skin that fell from their hosts. Then human beings invented rugs and carpets, which were made from wool—a type of animal hair. Carpet beetles moved in with people soon afterward, and the grubs have been munching on home furnishings ever since. Grubs feed for about a month before turning into adult beetles. They fly away to find a mate and then lay eggs near a good supply of food—such as a new carpet.

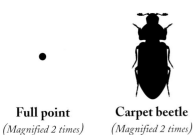

Full point
(Magnified 2 times)

Carpet beetle
(Magnified 2 times)

SIZE COMPARISON

▶ CARPET BEETLE GRUBS are known as "woolly bears" because their bodies are covered in long, shaggy, furlikespines, called setae.

Diet of a Carpet Beetle

Carpet beetles eat anything made from keratin. This is the protein found in hair, feathers, and fingernails. Waxy layers of keratin also help to keep skin waterproof. Carpet beetles will even eat holes in leather, which is made from the toughened skin of cows and other large animals.

Did you know?

• Carpet beetles live in violin cases and eat the long hairs on the bow.

• The beetles are used in museums to clean away the scraps of dead skin and flesh from animal skeletons before they are put on display.

• Adult carpet beetles clean up after spiders by eating up the dried husks left dangling in webs.

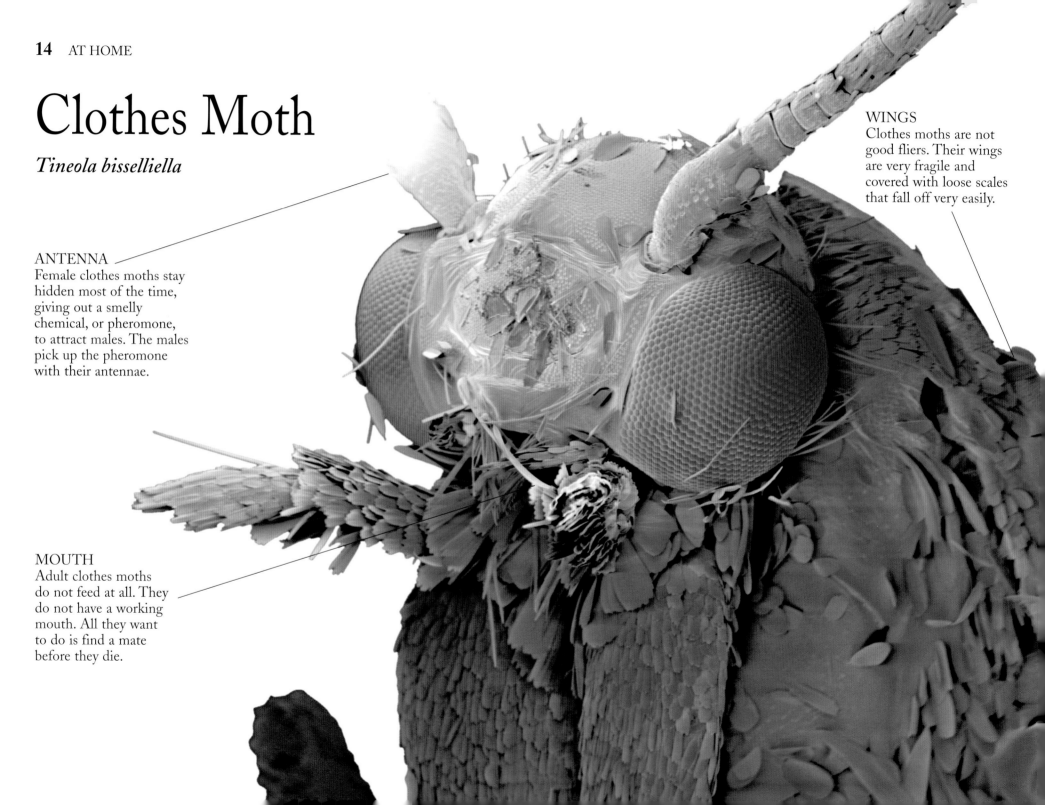

Clothes Moth

Tineola bisselliella

ANTENNA
Female clothes moths stay hidden most of the time, giving out a smelly chemical, or pheromone, to attract males. The males pick up the pheromone with their antennae.

MOUTH
Adult clothes moths do not feed at all. They do not have a working mouth. All they want to do is find a mate before they die.

WINGS
Clothes moths are not good fliers. Their wings are very fragile and covered with loose scales that fall off very easily.

Clothes moths are bad fliers, but that has not stopped them being world travelers. By hitching a ride on people's clothes, these small, drab moths have set up home in all corners of the globe. And they are a pest wherever they end up, chewing holes in fine clothes. Their little caterpillars are the main offenders. They munch their way through anything made from animal fibers, especially wool, but also silk and even feathered hats. They may flutter off if you get too near, but they are more likely to run for the nearest hiding place.

Full point
(Magnified 3 times)

Clothes moth
(Magnified 3 times)

SIZE COMPARISON

▶ ADULT CLOTHES MOTH are about ½in (1cm) long, and you are most likely to see males resting on the wall. When it is time to develop into an adult moth, the caterpillars build a case from the fibers of clothes, making a fluffy cocoon that is perfectly camouflaged.

Protect your Wardrobe

Being infested with clothes moths can be very expensive because they ruin your clothes. One way to protect your wardrobe is to put some mothballs in it. These are made from waxy chemicals that give off a sharp-smelling vapor that kills the moths—but they also make your clothes smell funny.

Did you know?

• A good way to kill any moth caterpillars in your clothing is to wrap it all in plastic and put it in the freezer for a few weeks. The insects die of cold.

• Cedar wood gives off a gas similar to that produced by mothballs, so precious fabrics are sometimes stored in chests made from cedar.

Cockroach

Periplaneta americana

MOUTH
A cockroach's mouth is ready
for anything. It can chew up
just about any type of food.

NECK SHIELD
A thick shield behind the head
protects the soft body underneath. The
delicate hind wings are also covered by
the tougher forewings.

CLAWS
Roaches will climb just
about anywhere thanks
to claws on the tips of
their long legs.

LONG ANTENNAE
The cockroach cannot
see much in the dark,
so it feels its way with
long antennae.

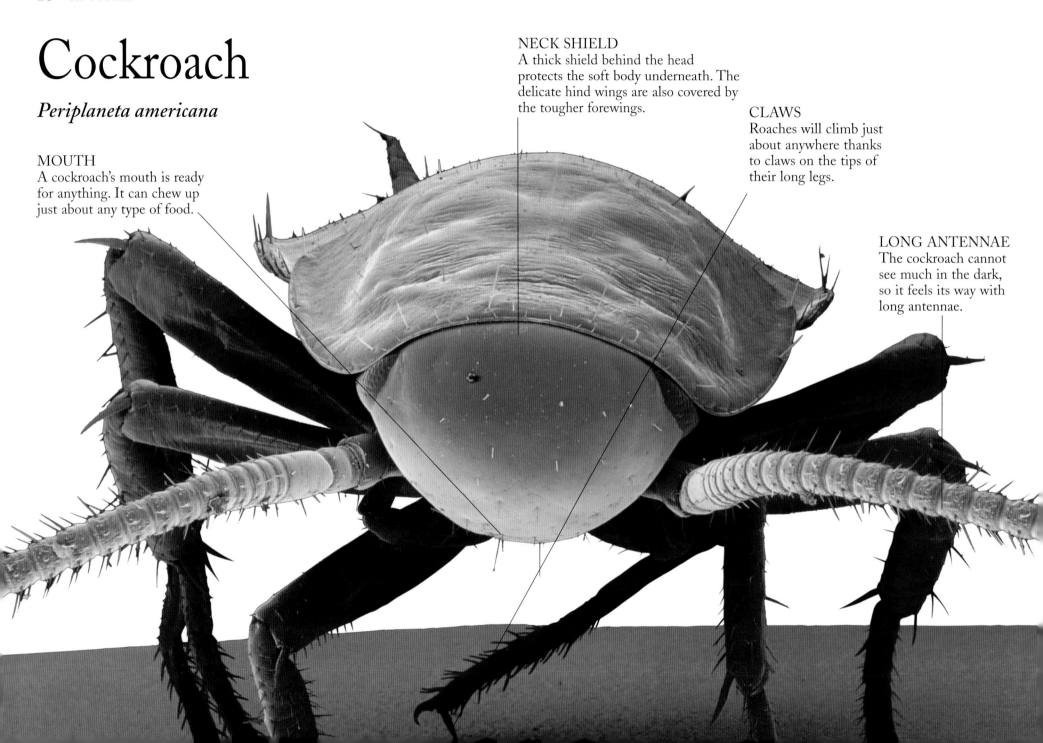

Yuck! It's a cockroach! Seeing one of these tough bugs scuttle up a wall or across a floor is never good news. Cockroaches live in dirty places, surviving on rotten food—or something worse. They stay out of sight during the day, wedged into dark nooks and crannies. When the lights go out, the roaches emerge—often in large numbers. Cockroaches can breed very quickly. The females often carry their eggs with them in a protective case. One pair of cockroaches could multiply into seven million roaches in just one year. The baby roaches, or nymphs, are wingless but otherwise look and live a lot like their parents.

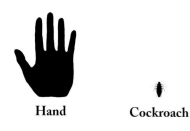

Hand　　　**Cockroach**

SIZE COMPARISON

▶ IF THERE IS SOME leftover food around, a cockroach will find it. Some species of roach do not live wild any more, but survive only alongside humans. These pests have developed resistance to chemical sprays intended to wipe them out.

Space Travel

Cockroaches get everywhere, even on board spacecraft. The insects are tough enough for space travel: They can survive for four hours without oxygen and go for a month without eating. In 2008, Russian scientists found that space cockroaches grow faster and are stronger than those back on Earth.

Did you know?

• A cockroach eats almost anything—including the droppings of another cockroach.

• The ancestors of cockroaches from more than 300 million years ago were one of the first types of flying insect.

Crane Fly

Tipulidae

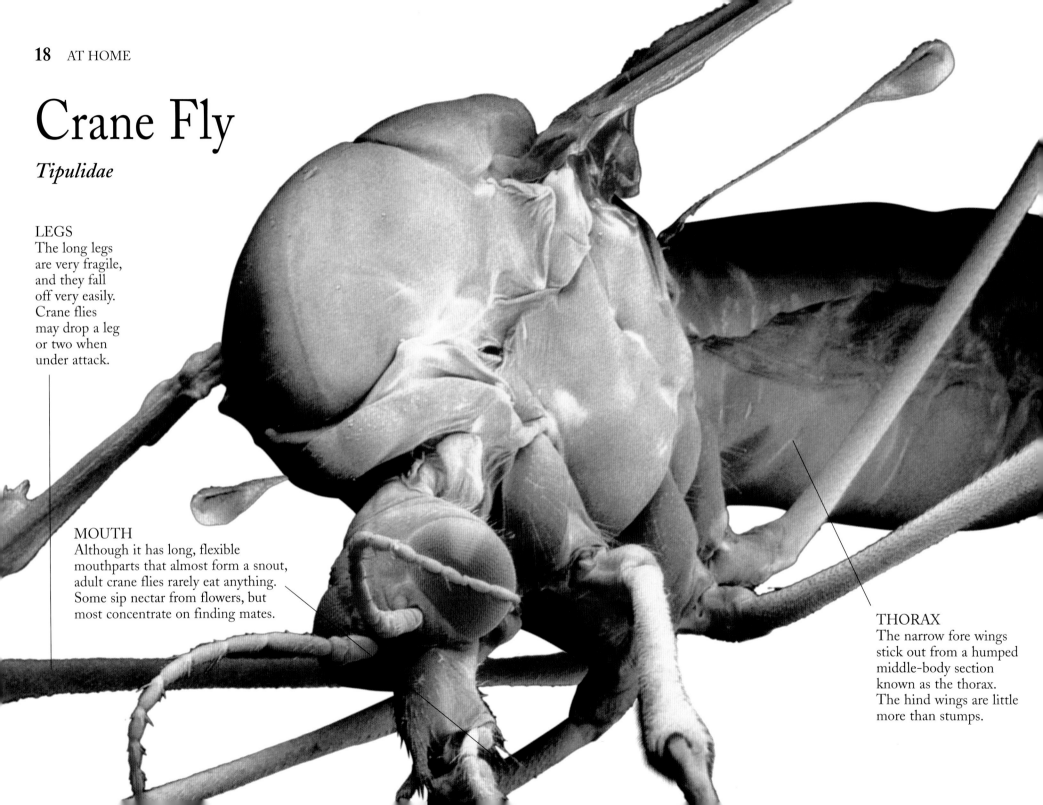

LEGS
The long legs are very fragile, and they fall off very easily. Crane flies may drop a leg or two when under attack.

MOUTH
Although it has long, flexible mouthparts that almost form a snout, adult crane flies rarely eat anything. Some sip nectar from flowers, but most concentrate on finding mates.

THORAX
The narrow fore wings stick out from a humped middle-body section known as the thorax. The hind wings are little more than stumps.

These gangly flies are all legs and fluttering wings. In some parts of the world, they are better known as a daddy long-legs. Other people know them as gollywhoppers or gallinippers. Like all types of fly, crane flies have only two wings. The wings are long and narrow, so the insects are very clumsy flyers. They are most active at night and often get trapped inside houses at dusk, crashing into lights and windows in an attempt to escape. However, not all crane flies are spindly flappers like this. A tiny species from the Rocky Mountains grows no wings at all and lives in the snow.

Hand

Crane fly

SIZE COMPARISON

▶ SOME NICKNAMES, SUCH as mosquito hawk or skeeter eater, suggest that crane flies are hunters or like to bite people. However, these large insects are harmless.

Leatherjackets

The maggots of crane flies are called leatherjackets. They live underground, eating roots. A lawn infested with leatherjackets will develop bald patches of earth, where the unseen insects have killed the grasses. Leatherjackets are a big problem for farmers and ground staff looking after sports fields.

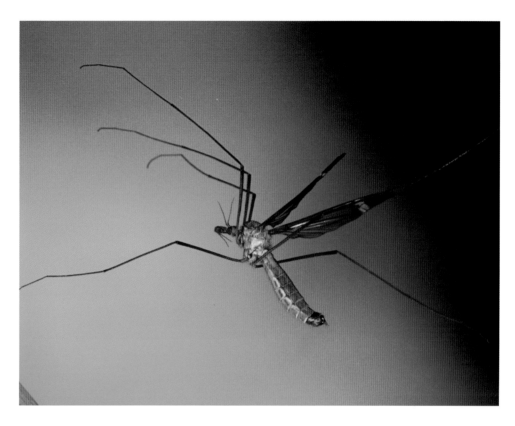

Did you know?

• A male crane fly has a square tip to its abdomen; the female's is pointed.

• Australian crane flies are colored to look like a large stinging wasp. Insect-hunting birds normally leave them alone.

• Some crane flies hide from predators by hanging from spiders' webs pretending to be twigs.

Daddy Long-Legs Spider

Pholcidae

EYES
The spider has six eyes arranged in two triangles on top of the head. The main pair of eyes face forward to look at what the spider is about to eat.

ABDOMEN
When raiding another spider's web, the daddy long-legs spider taps on the silk with its abdomen. The other spider scuttles over to see what is happening and ends up as the invader's next meal.

FANGS
The spider's two fangs inject a poison that paralyzes prey—but the victim is often still alive when the spider begins to eat.

This spider gets its names for it long spindly legs. Although its name sounds a little funny, a daddy long-legs spider is a very skilled hunter. It lives in damp parts of the house—another name for it is cellar spider—and builds webs out of sheets of silk. When an insect blunders into the web, their struggles make them more tangled. The daddy long-legs then fires extra lines of silk over its victim, trapping it. Once it is tied up, the spider steps in and delivers a poisonous bite. A daddy long-legs spider will also raid the web of another spider, stealing its catch or eating any eggs.

Hand　　**Daddy long-legs spider**

SIZE COMPARISON

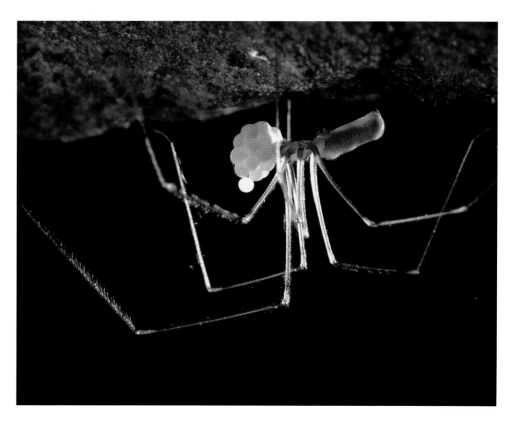

▶ FEMALE SPIDERS CARRY their round eggs in a bag made from strands of silk. She holds the bag with her pedipalps making it hard to feed while the eggs develop.

Defense Display

The fangs of a daddy long-legs are only small and too short to give a larger animal much of a nip. So, in its defense, the spider puts on an extraordinary display. It trembles so that the whole web shakes wildly, and spins itself spins around so fast that it becomes a whirly blur—enough to put off any attacker.

Did you know?

• Daddy long-legs spiders are also called skull spiders because the markings on the abdomen look a little like a human skull.

• Unlike most spider's webs, the silk used in the web of a daddy long-legs spider is not sticky.

• Thanks to their very long legs, these spiders do not get stuck in the webs of other spiders. They always have a few feet free to pull themselves clear.

Dust Mite

Dermatophagoides pteronyssinus

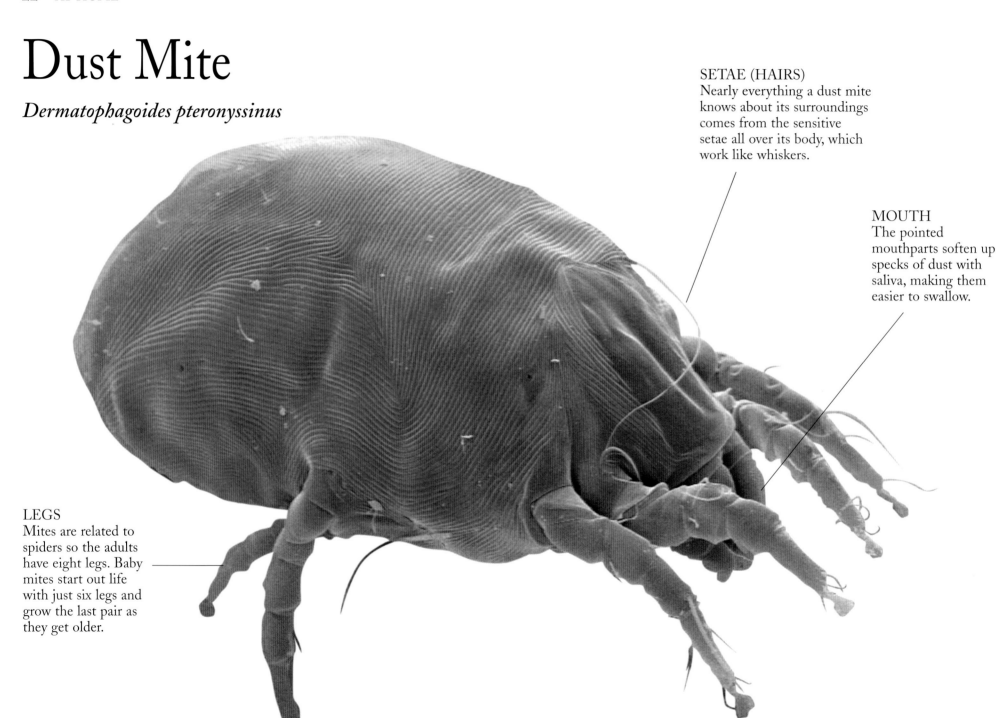

SETAE (HAIRS)
Nearly everything a dust mite knows about its surroundings comes from the sensitive setae all over its body, which work like whiskers.

MOUTH
The pointed mouthparts soften up specks of dust with saliva, making them easier to swallow.

LEGS
Mites are related to spiders so the adults have eight legs. Baby mites start out life with just six legs and grow the last pair as they get older.

Y ou are not alone—you share your home with millions of other animals. You cannot see them, even with a magnifying glass, but dust mites are living all over your house. They especially love thick carpets or luxuriously soft furniture. The mites couldn't live without you. In fact, they survive by eating little bits of you—specks of your dead skin that settle as fine dust around your home. They eat each particle several times until they've got all the nourishment possible— and its the chemicals from their gut, remaining on the particles, that cause allergic reactions. Makes you feel itchy just thinking about it!

Full point
(Magnified 10 times)

Dust mite
(Magnified 10 times)

SIZE COMPARISON

▶ DUST BALLS ARE a feast to dust mites. These are made up of strands of human hairs and fibers from clothes and carpets with much tinier specks mixed in. Some specks are the remains of household insects. But most of them are flakes of human skin: We shed the outer layer of our skin every two days.

Invisible Mites

Human dust mites can live in their millions inside pillows, mattresses, and cushions. The invisible mites are to blame for many people suffering from asthma, rashes, and other allergies. The chemicals used in a mite's stomach to digest its dusty food come out in its droppings. These chemicals get into the air of dusty rooms and irritate people's lungs, eyes, and noses.

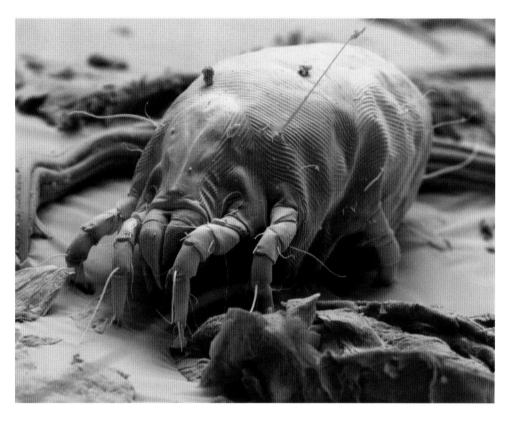

Did you know?

• Mites do not have a stomach. Instead, their gut is a simple tube with a few dead-end branches leading off of it.

• Dust mites spread through the house on tiny swirling air currents created as people move around.

• Mites could have been one of the first land animals. Fossils have been found from 400 million years ago.

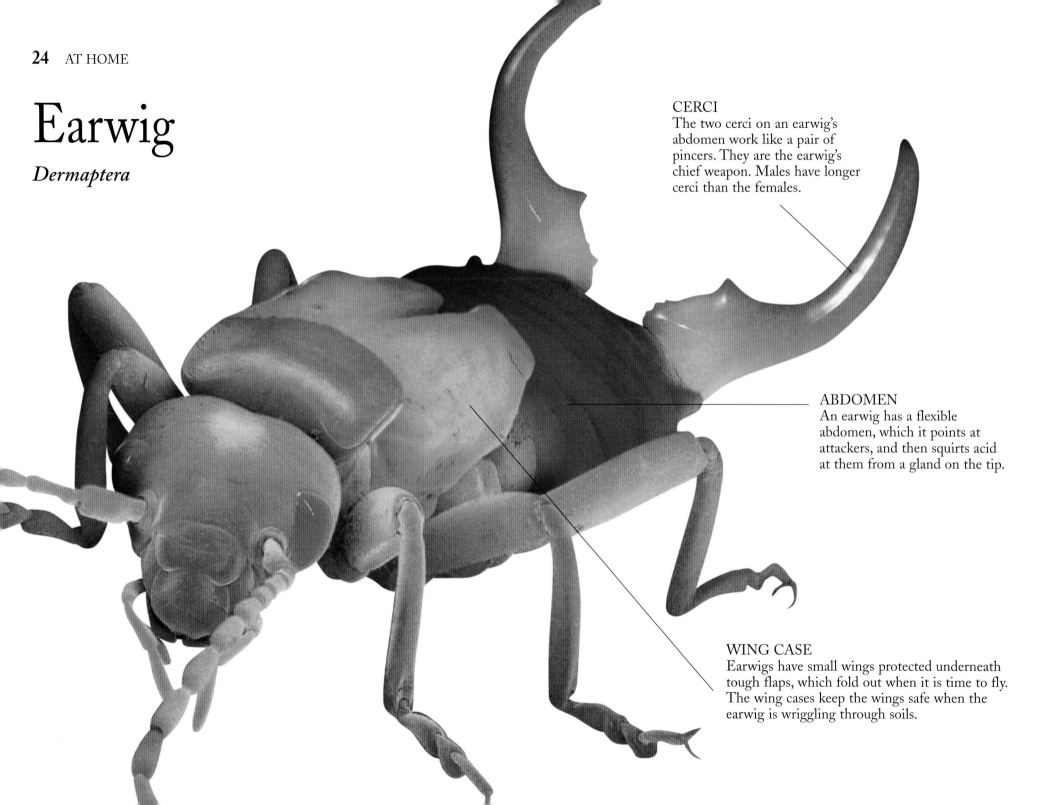

Earwig

Dermaptera

CERCI
The two cerci on an earwig's abdomen work like a pair of pincers. They are the earwig's chief weapon. Males have longer cerci than the females.

ABDOMEN
An earwig has a flexible abdomen, which it points at attackers, and then squirts acid at them from a gland on the tip.

WING CASE
Earwigs have small wings protected underneath tough flaps, which fold out when it is time to fly. The wing cases keep the wings safe when the earwig is wriggling through soils.

People used to think that an earwig likes to crawl into a person's ear when he or she is asleep and lays their eggs—or worse, slice through the eardrum with its tail pincers! Thankfully, this is just a very tall tale. However, earwigs do like dark, damp spots and often turn up inside plant pots and muddy boots. Earwigs come out at night to hunt, using the clasps on the tail to grab small insects and mites. Even the longest pincers cannot hurt a person, but earwigs use them to scare off other attackers. Males also fight each other with their pincers in long duels over mates. This explains their other name, which is pincerbug.

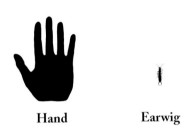

Hand   **Earwig**

SIZE COMPARISON

▶ EARWIG EGGS ARE under attack from worms and molds, and tiny flies want to lay their own eggs inside. Earwig mothers clean away any dirt from the smooth eggs and stop them from drying out.

Caring Parents

Most insects never see their young, but earwigs are very caring parents. The mother digs a den in the ground for her eggs. She stands guard over them until the tiny nymphs hatch out. Mother then feeds the nymphs by bringing up some of her last meal. But when it is time to leave home, the nymphs have to move quickly. Their hungry mother soon forgets who they are and may eat one of the stragglers!

Did you know?

• The world's largest earwig lives on the tiny island of St. Helena in the Atlantic Ocean. It is very rare, but can grow as long a man's finger.

• Scientists think that the length of a male earwig's cerci depends on how much good food his mother gave him after he hatched from the egg.

• Earwig mean "ear insect" in Old English. Earwig wings form an ear shape when they are spread. Perhaps that explains how the bug got its name.

Housefly

Musca domestica

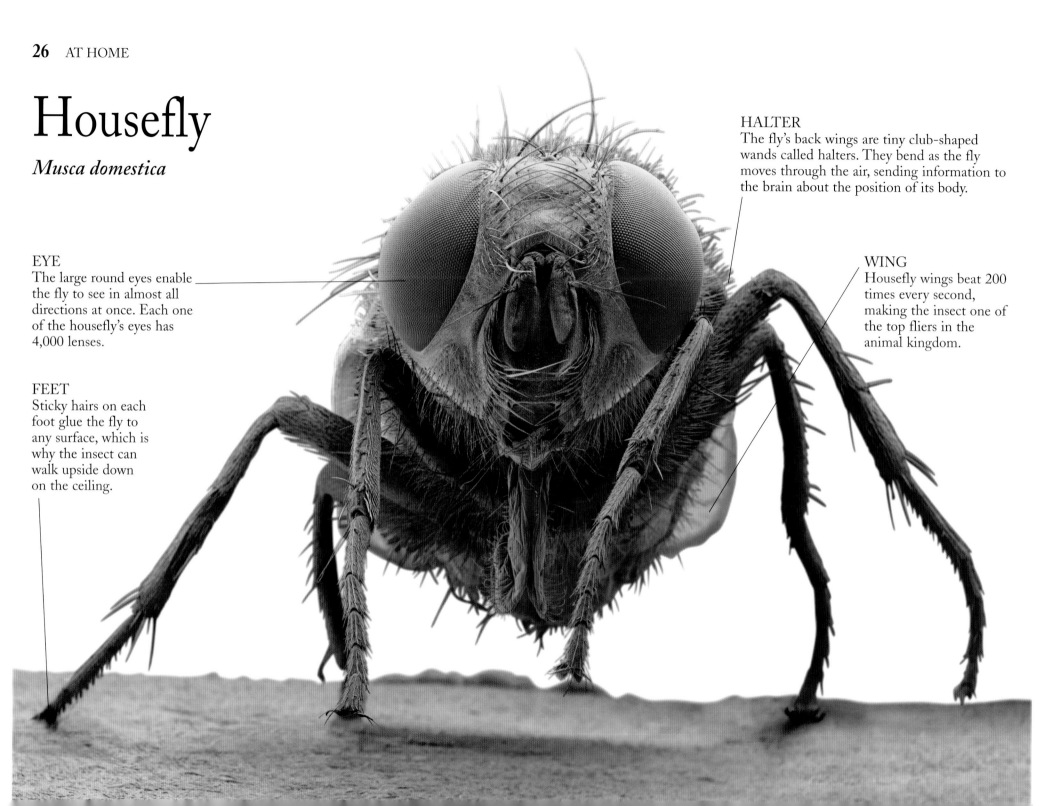

HALTER
The fly's back wings are tiny club-shaped wands called halters. They bend as the fly moves through the air, sending information to the brain about the position of its body.

EYE
The large round eyes enable the fly to see in almost all directions at once. Each one of the housefly's eyes has 4,000 lenses.

WING
Housefly wings beat 200 times every second, making the insect one of the top fliers in the animal kingdom.

FEET
Sticky hairs on each foot glue the fly to any surface, which is why the insect can walk upside down on the ceiling.

S plat! There goes another housefly. Before you swat your next fly, take a look at what is one of the wonders of the insect world. They are less than ½in (1cm) long, but can fly at about 3mph (5km/h). That is half a million body lengths in just 60 minutes! A man-sized fly would travel as fast as a jet fighter! But it is not good to have too many of these super-flies living in your house. They spread stomach bugs and more serious diseases. And it take just 10 days for one housefly egg to become a full-sized adult. In six months, a single housefly could multiply into 5 trillion more! So, get swatting!

Full point
(Magnified 2 times)

Housefly
(Magnified 2 times)

SIZE COMPARISON

▶ HOUSEFLIES TASTE WITH their feet, so they know if something is good to eat as soon as they land on it. They squirt a blob of stomach juice onto food, which turns the food into a goo.

Kaleidoscope Vision

Houseflies see things very differently to us. Each of their eye lenses makes it own image, so to a fly the world looks a bit like it does when we look through a kaleidoscope. Having so many views of the world enables the fly to spot tiny movements—and that's why it's able to buzz off long before your flyswatter gets anywhere near it.

Did you know?

• Houseflies cannot bite—but similar flies can. If the one you are looking at has red eyes, you are probably safe.

• Houseflies spread diseases by leaving vomit on our food.

• To land on a ceiling, a housefly has to do a body flip.

House Spider

Tegenaria domestica

PEDIPALPS
This male house spider
has larger pedipalps
than a female. The palps
are sensitive feelers and
the male uses them
during mating.

LEGS
Male house spiders have longer
legs than females—they have a
lot farther to walk in their search
for mates.

EYES
House spiders have eight eyes. The
largest pair point forward, while the
six smaller ones also look sideways.

If you see a spider going for a walk around your home, it is almost certainly a male house spider looking for a mate. The female spiders never move far from their funnel-shaped cobwebs. It may look messy, but the web is a deadly trap. When an insect wanders into the wide entrance, it triggers trip wires made of tight, sticky threads.

The threads tug the insect into the heart of the web, where the hungry spider is waiting. Like all spiders, house spiders cannot chew, so they pump stomach juices into their victims. These juices digest the prey's body into a fleshy soup, which the spider sucks up.

Full point
(Magnified 2 times)

House spider
(Magnified 2 times)

SIZE COMPARISON

▶ SPIDERS FIND IT difficult to grip smooth surfaces. If they wander into a bath or sink, they cannot escape. They are not dangerous and need help to get out before being washed way.

Hobo Spider

Ordinary house spiders are more or less harmless to people. However, their larger cousin, the hobo spider, can give a more painful bite. Hobo spiders come from Europe, where they rarely come indoors. However, some hobos made it over to North America in the 1920s. These new arrivals set up home in people's houses and have become a nasty pest.

Did you know?

• House spiders are close relatives of the black widow spider, a much more dangerous animal.

• After a male house spider has found a mate, he dies—and the female eats him.

• A house with several spiders will have fewer annoying insects.

Mange Mite

Sarcoptidae

FOOT
The mite has suckers on its feet to cling to hair and skin.

HAPPY COUPLE
Male mange mites are half the size of the females. The mites mate only once—that is enough for the female to lay eggs for the rest of her life.

DOMED BODY
Mites are related to spiders but have only one body section—not two. The rounded body enables them to crawl around under the skin.

Have you ever had an itch you cannot scratch? Just imagine what it is like for a pet dog with mange. Mange is an itching disease caused by microscopic mites that live on the hairs and skin. In fact, some mites dig into and through the skin. Every dog has a few mites living on it, but as long as the dog stays healthy, its body can fight off attacks by the mites. But if the dog gets sick or does not get enough to eat, the mites begin to win the battle. Mangy dogs get bald patches and are always scratching at crusty sores on the skin. It is rare that a dog's mites spread to a human—but it is not impossible!

Full point
(Magnified 10 times)

Mange mite
(Magnified 10 times)

SIZE COMPARISON

▶ THE WORST KIND of mange is caused by mites that live in burrows under the dog's skin. The females lay their eggs inside, and baby mites dig their way out.

Care for your Pet

It is not just pet dogs that suffer from mange. Cats can get it too. In fact, it is very common for little kittens and puppies to have a bit of trouble from mites when they are young. However, if they are fed properly and well looked after, they soon grow out of the problem.

Did you know?

• Dogs with mange develop a scratching reflex. If you stroke their ear, they lift up the back leg for a scratch.

• Vets can use medicines to kill the mites, although border collies and similar sheep dog breeds must never have the drugs because it attacks their brains!

• Dogs can pick up the worst strains of mange from wild foxes and coyotes.

Silverfish

Thysanura

SIX LEGS
Silverfish have six legs like an insect, but there are signs that early silverfish had many more.

ANTENNA
The long antennae are used as feelers and as chemical detectors for tasting scraps of food.

BRISTLETAILS
Silverfish have three bristly spines forming a tail.

Experts disagree whether silverfish are actually insects or some other kind of ancient critter from the dawn of life on land. Silverfish are so small and secretive that you may never see one. By day, they lurk in dark and damp nooks, and come out only in the dead of night to look for food. However, their idea of food is odd. They like to tuck into scraps of paper, lick the paste from behind wallpaper, and munch on the glue in books. They also feast on grains of sugar, flour, and other sweet foods spilled in the kitchen. When not feeding, silverfish look for mates. The males court the females with a little dance.

Full point
(Magnified 2 times)

Silverfish
(Magnified 2 times)

SIZE COMPARISON

▶ SILVERFISH ARE NAMED after the shiny scales covering their backs. They are also fast movers and flit across the floor if surprised by bright lights.

Smaller Versions of their Parents

Unlike most insects, silverfish do not change shape as they grow. The nymphs are just little versions of their parents. As it grows, a silverfish must molt—shed its stiff outer skin when it gets too small. Even adult silverfish molt from time to time, replacing their shiny scales. A tiny silverfish can live for eight years!

Did you know?

• Firebrats are a type of silverfish that love being warm. They can be found in cracks and crevices around an old-fashioned fireplace.

• The oldest insect fossil ever found is 400 million years old. It had a three-pronged bristletail a little like that of a silverfish.

Spider's Web

NIGHT WORK
Spiders normally spin
their webs at night, so
they are ready for the
rush of insects at dawn.

THIN THREADS
Spider's silk is
incredibly thin;
3,000 threads laid
side by side would
be just about $\frac{1}{25}$in
(1mm) thick.

STRETCHY STRANDS
Spiders control how stretchy their
silk is. They use their strongest
threads to wrap up their prey to
stop it from struggling free.

Most micromonsters are too small to see—or are good at avoiding you. The most obvious signs of them are the webs they leave behind. Many insects use silk, but the best weavers are the spiders. At home, look in the corners of the ceilings and windows. You are sure to find at least a couple of old webs. Spiders' silk is twice as strong as a steel wire of the same thickness. It can stretch by a third before snapping. Most spider webs are for trapping flying insects. The prey is trapped by the sticky silk, while the spiders themselves stride across the web safely by standing on nonsticky threads.

Human

Spider's web

SIZE COMPARISON

▶ A SPIDER OFTEN uses a gentle breeze to start a web. The air wafts a fine thread across an open space, providing the first strut in the complex silk structure.

Using Silk

Silk starts out as a liquid. The spider squirts it through tiny holes in its spinning organs, or spinnerets. As soon as the liquid silk meets the air, it begins to harden into a stretchy thread. The spider collects each thread with its back legs and pays it out behind. As well as making webs, spiders use silk to make a case for their eggs or as safety ropes when climbing.

Did you know?

• Tiny spiders travel by air using a few strands of silk trailing from their behinds to catch the wind.

• The strongest webs are made by orb-web spiders. These can hold 1,000 times their own weight!

• In 2009, a piece of cloth about 10 x 3ft (3 x 1m) was woven from spider's silk in Madagascar. It contained the silk of one million spiders.

Wood Termite

Coptotermes niger

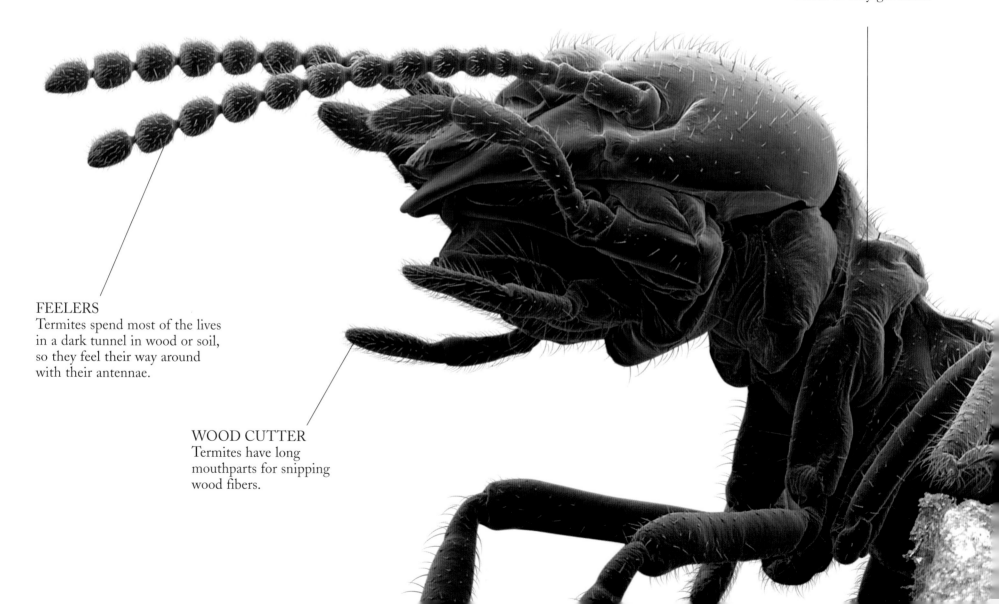

BASIC BODIES
Termites have simple bodies. They do not change much as they get older.

FEELERS
Termites spend most of the lives in a dark tunnel in wood or soil, so they feel their way around with their antennae.

WOOD CUTTER
Termites have long mouthparts for snipping wood fibers.

As their name suggest, wood termites live on wood. They tunnel away inside the beams of houses. Eventually the wood becomes so hollow and weak that people fall through the floor, and a house can actually fall down! The termites swallow the wood, but it is not their food. Bacteria and other germs in their stomachs turn the wood into a mush. The termites use their woody droppings to build gardens inside the nest. A fungus grows on the droppings, which is the termites' real food. And if they fancy something different to eat, they eat the bodies of any of their brothers and sisters who have died recently!

Full point
(Magnified 2 times)

Termite
(Magnified 2 times)

SIZE COMPARISON

▶ PEST CONTROLLERS USE sensitive microphones to find wood termites. The machine can pick up the sound of the insects munching inside the wood.

Not Ants

Termites are also called white ants because they live in large colonies and work together to build nests and find food. However, termites are not ants, and their colonies are very different. The nest is ruled by a queen termite who lays all the eggs. However, unlike ants, there is also a king termite. He is the father of every termite in the kingdom. The king and queen's children grow into small workers or large soldiers who defend the nest. Even the nymphs help out.

Did you know?

• Some soldier ants are filled with sticky liquid. When the nest is under attack by ants, the soldiers explode their entire bodies, spraying the attackers with glue.

• A queen termite can lay thousands of eggs in one day. She is so large that she can no longer move.

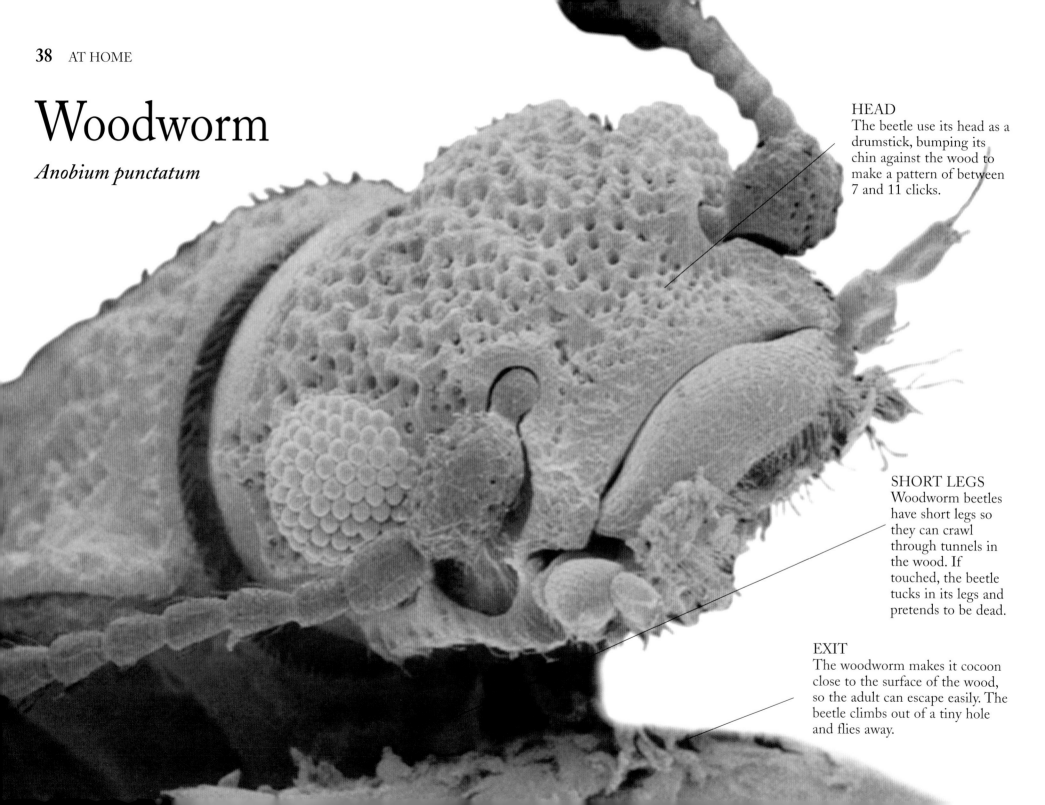

Woodworm

Anobium punctatum

HEAD
The beetle use its head as a drumstick, bumping its chin against the wood to make a pattern of between 7 and 11 clicks.

SHORT LEGS
Woodworm beetles have short legs so they can crawl through tunnels in the wood. If touched, the beetle tucks in its legs and pretends to be dead.

EXIT
The woodworm makes it cocoon close to the surface of the wood, so the adult can escape easily. The beetle climbs out of a tiny hole and flies away.

Woodworms are the grubs of tiny beetles that gnaw through wood. They leave a warren of tunnels that weaken the wood so much that old chairs can suddenly give way. Once a woodworm has its fill of food, it forms a cocoon in the same way a caterpillar does. Inside, the grub turns into an adult beetle. The beetle then digs its way out and goes in search of a mate. It bumps on the wood to make a rapid clicking call, which attracts other beetles. In the past, people often heard this while sitting in silence around a deathbed. That is why woodworms are also called deathwatch beetles.

Full point
(Magnified 2 times)

Woodworm
(Magnified 2 times)

SIZE COMPARISON

▶ WOODWORMS CREATE A tell-tale pattern of tunnels in wood. You can sometimes see them after a tree trunk has been cut into planks—especially on old floorboards. The insects can be dealt with using chemicals, and most of the tunnels do not weaken the board much.

Slow-grower

It can take years for a woodworm to grow up. Wood is not very good food, and so the grubs grow slowly. The grubs release more goodness from the food with the help of bacteria in their stomachs. The germs live in little sacs, which work like tiny compost heaps, slowly breaking the sawdust down into sugar.

Did you know?

• The female beetles lay their eggs on cracks in wood. When they hatch, the tiny woodworms will burrow inside.

• Woodworm beetles have some strange relatives. The tobacco beetle lives in cigarette packs while the drugstore beetle nibbles through the pills in a pharmacy.

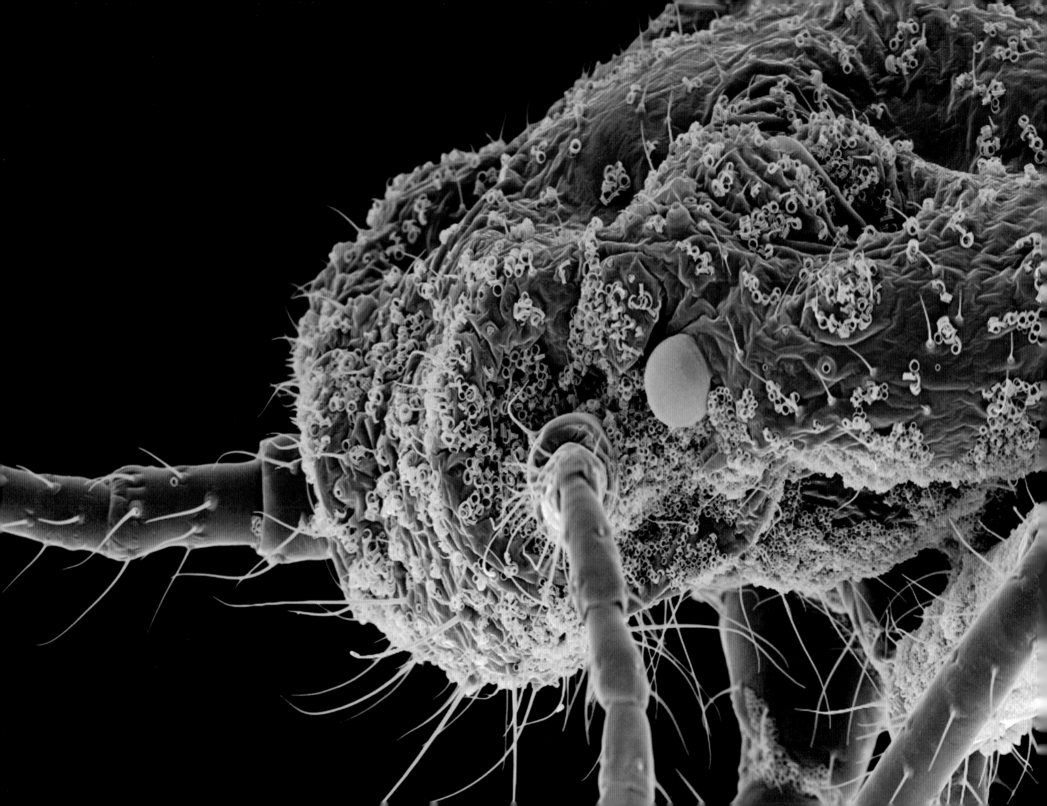

Food Bugs

EVERYONE HAS GOT TO EAT. And that includes this group of micromonsters. The problem, though, is that they like to eat all the same foods as we do, and they can be a real pest. Some of them are the enemy of farmers—they attack crops growing in fields and can destroy a whole year's worth of food. In the past, an attack of these food bugs would have been a disaster. People have starved to death for that very reason. Today, we are better equipped to deal with the pesky insects. In a few cases, people have learned to love the bugs. The food doesn't taste right without them!

Farmers use chemicals to kill the pests in the fields, but once the food is ready to eat it is too late to spray poisons on it. So people have come up with ingenious ways of keeping stores of food safe from the destructive micromonsters. They unleash armies of killer wasps to guard the food or spray fake smells to lure the bugs into traps. Thankfully, our food is cleaner than it has ever been, so the meal on your plate is sure to be free of bugs. Take a look at what you're missing.

Colorado Potato Beetle

Leptinotarsa decemlineata

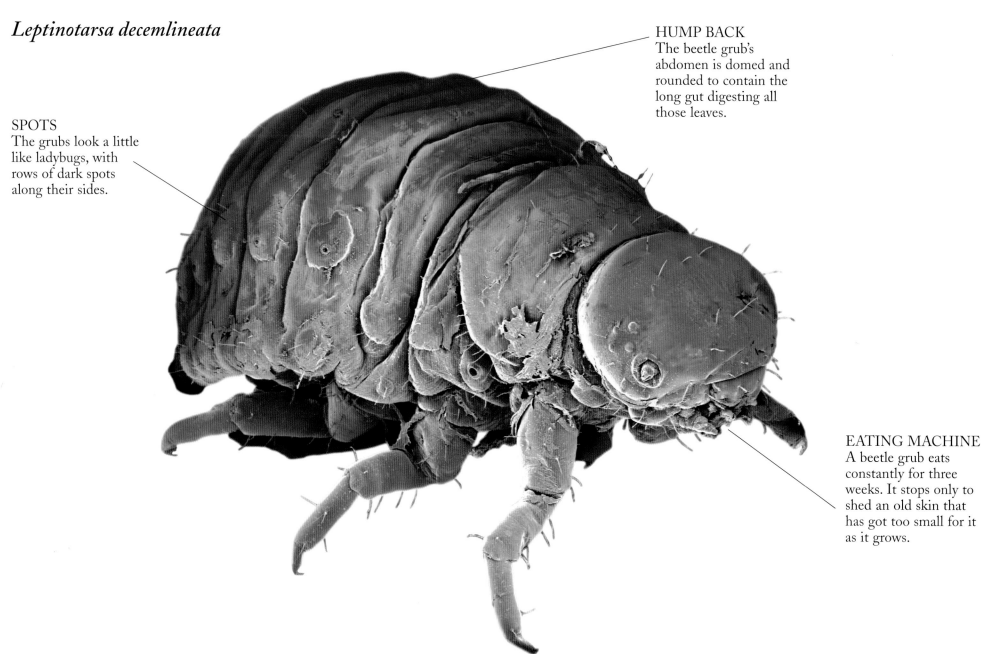

HUMP BACK
The beetle grub's abdomen is domed and rounded to contain the long gut digesting all those leaves.

SPOTS
The grubs look a little like ladybugs, with rows of dark spots along their sides.

EATING MACHINE
A beetle grub eats constantly for three weeks. It stops only to shed an old skin that has got too small for it as it grows.

The potato is an American vegetable, first grown by farmers in Peru about 5,000 years ago. One of the worst potato pests also comes from America. The Colorado potato beetle used to eat a tumbleweed called buffalo burr, which grows in Mexico and the western United States. When potatoes arrived in the area 200 years ago, the beetles' grubs turned their attention to potato leaves, wrecking entire fields of the valuable crop. In the 1870s, the beetle sneaked across the Atlantic and spread through the potato farms of Europe. Colorado potato beetles now live across Asia all the way to the Pacific Ocean.

Full point

(Magnified 2 times)

Colorado potato beetle

(Magnified 2 times)

SIZE COMPARISON

▶ ADULT COLORADO BEETLES are only ½in (1cm) long, but they are easy to identify because of the 10 stripes running along the back. The beetle is also known as the ten-striped spearman.

A Poisonous Meal

Potato leaves are full of poisons. People can only stomach the plant's swollen underground tubers, but potato beetle grubs can withstand the nasty chemicals in the rest of the plant. The beetles are also resistant to many of the poisons in pesticide sprays designed to kill the insects before they damage crops.

Did you know?

• The Incas of Peru kept their potatoes safe from pests by freezing them in high mountain ice caves.

• Farmers have tried to kill potato beetles by infecting them with fungus and unleashing swarms of parasitic flies.

• Colorado potato beetles also attack tomato and eggplant crops.

Blowfly

Calliphora vicina

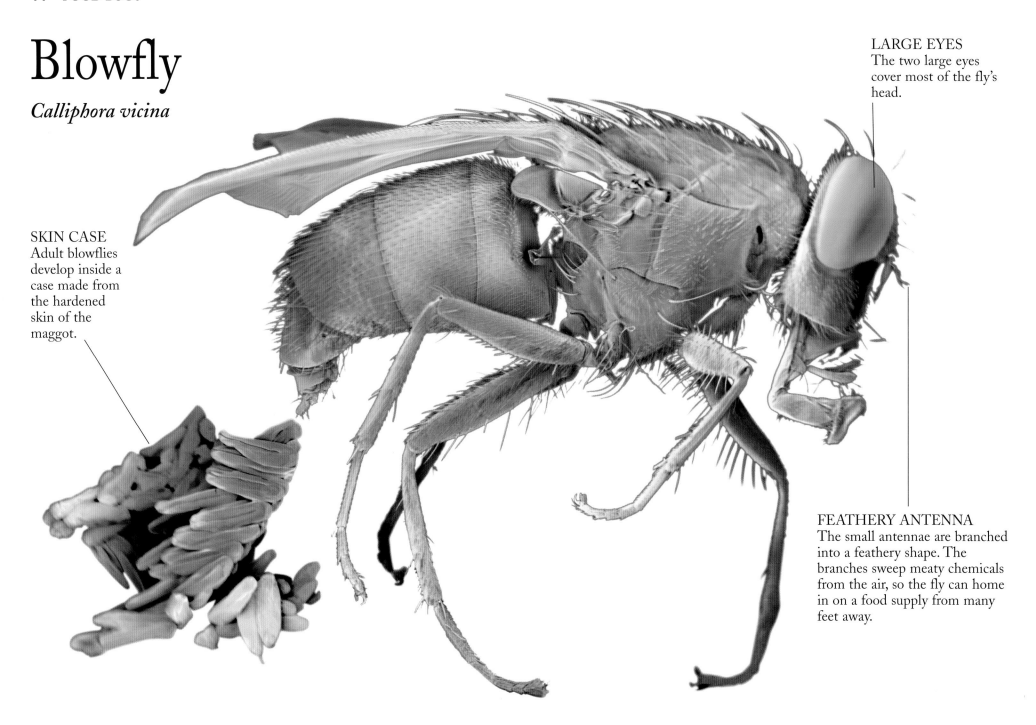

LARGE EYES
The two large eyes cover most of the fly's head.

SKIN CASE
Adult blowflies develop inside a case made from the hardened skin of the maggot.

FEATHERY ANTENNA
The small antennae are branched into a feathery shape. The branches sweep meaty chemicals from the air, so the fly can home in on a food supply from many feet away.

These bristled flies are on a mission to find meat. The flesh of an animal is the perfect nursery for their babies—whether it's fresh meat left in a kitchen or the rotting corpse of a wild animal. Within days, the meat will be full of maggots gorging on the flesh. Then they wriggle into a quiet nook, to become a pupa, from which the adult fly emerges. Adult males sip flower nectar, but females need protein to make eggs, and feast on meat and dung. Some blowfly maggots need living food— screwworms burrow into the faces of cattle, while sheep strike maggots hide under a sheep's thick fleece.

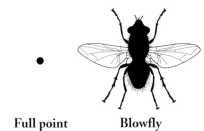

Full point	**Blowfly**
(Magnified 2 times)	*(Magnified 2 times)*

SIZE COMPARISON

▶ ADULT BLOWFLIES OFTEN look like they are wearing colorful glassy armor. As a result, they are often better known as blue- or greenbottles.

Clues to a Crime

Detectives look for blowfly maggots on murder victims to figure out when they died. Blowflies lay their eggs on human bodies within 48 hours of death. Experts measure the length of the maggots on the body and can tell how long they have been feeding there. If they find blowfly pupa near the body, that means the unfortunate victim died about two weeks before.

Did you know?

• The name "blow fly" may have been invented by William Shakespeare. It stems from being the older phrase "fly blown," which describes something that is riddled with fly eggs.

• Tropical plants fool blowflies into visiting them by giving off meaty scents. The flies transfer pollen between the flowers—or are trapped and dissolved by the plant.

• The nasty sounding Congo floor maggot drinks human blood! But it can't climb into a bed, so it will only attack people sleeping on the floor.

Cheese Mite

Tyrophagus casei

ROUNDED BODIES
The mites have simple rounded bodies and short legs, so they can wriggle around in tight spaces.

AIR TRAVEL
Cheese mites are too small to see without a magnifying glass. They are so light they can be carried around by air currents until they land on cheese or another type of food.

BURROWERS
Cheese mites eat their way into the surface of the cheese, producing tiny tubes lined with the tell-tale dust.

Imagine finding some gray-brown dust on a tasty piece of cheese. You wipe the dust away on the plate, and slice off a chunk. After you have finished eating your meal, you may notice that the dust from the cheese has gone for a walk. Don't be alarmed. It is just some harmless cheese mites. Actually cheese mite are pretty rare on food at home, but they are a problem for cheesemakers because they change the way the finished cheese tastes. Despite their name, the mites also eat a lot of other things, including cured meats, such as ham, and flour. It takes a lot of mites to produce the dust you see.

Full point
(Magnified 10 times)

Cheese mite
(Magnified 10 times)

SIZE COMPARISON

▶ SOME HARD CHEESES are considered ready to eat only when the surface is covered in a gray dust of dead mites! This gives the cheese a sweet minty flavor.

Making cheese

The people of Würchwitz, Germany, have built a statue of a cheese mite to honor the bug's role in making *Milbenkäse,* the local "mite cheese." Some say that eating mite cheese may reduce asthma and other allergies caused by dust mites, because it gives the body a chance to get used to the chemicals made by the creatures. The dust contains the living mites crawling over the dead bodies of older ones, covering them in their droppings.

Did you know?

• Mites in flour can irritate the skin. The rash is known as baker's itch.

• Cheese mites starred in the first animal documentary made in 1903.

• Some cheeses are coated in paraffin wax to stop the mites from getting inside.

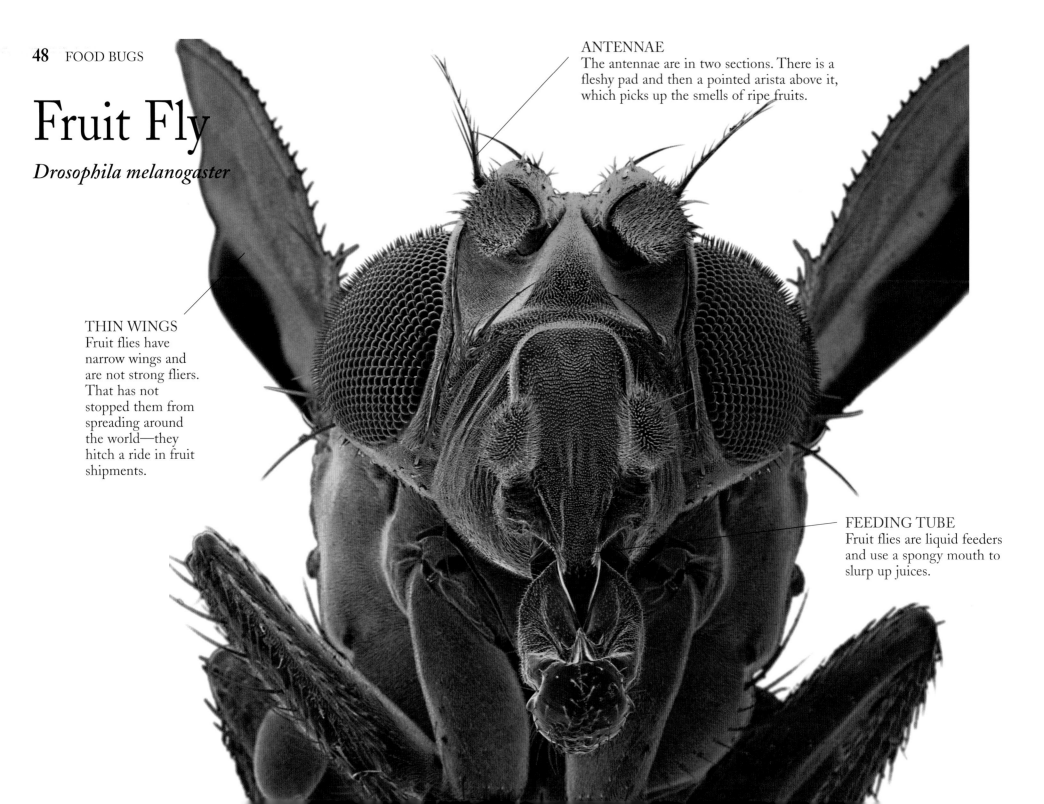

Fruit Fly

Drosophila melanogaster

ANTENNAE
The antennae are in two sections. There is a fleshy pad and then a pointed arista above it, which picks up the smells of ripe fruits.

THIN WINGS
Fruit flies have narrow wings and are not strong fliers. That has not stopped them from spreading around the world—they hitch a ride in fruit shipments.

FEEDING TUBE
Fruit flies are liquid feeders and use a spongy mouth to slurp up juices.

F ruit flies are tiny—just ¹⁄₁₆in (2mm) long, so small you may not even notice them. Unless, that is, there was ripe fruit nearby. Then they would swarm around it, sucking up its juices. Fruit flies can wreck fruit crops, especially juicy sweet summer fruits, such as peaches. The male produces a scent to attract mates, beating his wings to spread it through the air. Once a female has mated with him, she uses a sharp egg tube on her abdomen to cut through the fruit's skin and leave some eggs inside. The fly maggots hatching from the eggs feed on the pulp inside, and it does not take many to ruin a piece of fruit.

Full point
(Magnified 5 times)

Fruit fly
(Magnified 5 times)

SIZE COMPARISON

▶ ONE OF THE worst fruit pests is the medfly. Once from Africa, this colorful little insect now attacks orange groves, peach orchards, and coffee plantations around the world.

Science's Little Helpers

Fruit flies may be the enemy of farmers, but they are very useful for scientists who study genes. The flies breed very quickly. They also have enormous chromosomes (gene carriers) in their saliva glands, which are easy to study. Scientists have created many man-made versions of fruit flies with odd-shaped wings and strange eyes, which helps them figure out how a gene's directions are used to make a living body.

Did you know?

• Vinegar flies are fruit flies that like fruit that is so ripe its sugary juices are turning sour. They also infest bakeries and breweries.

• Some fruit flies do a circling mating dance with their wings spread out. The scientists who first saw it were reminded of peacocks and named the insects peacock flies.

Grain Weevil

Sitophilus granarius

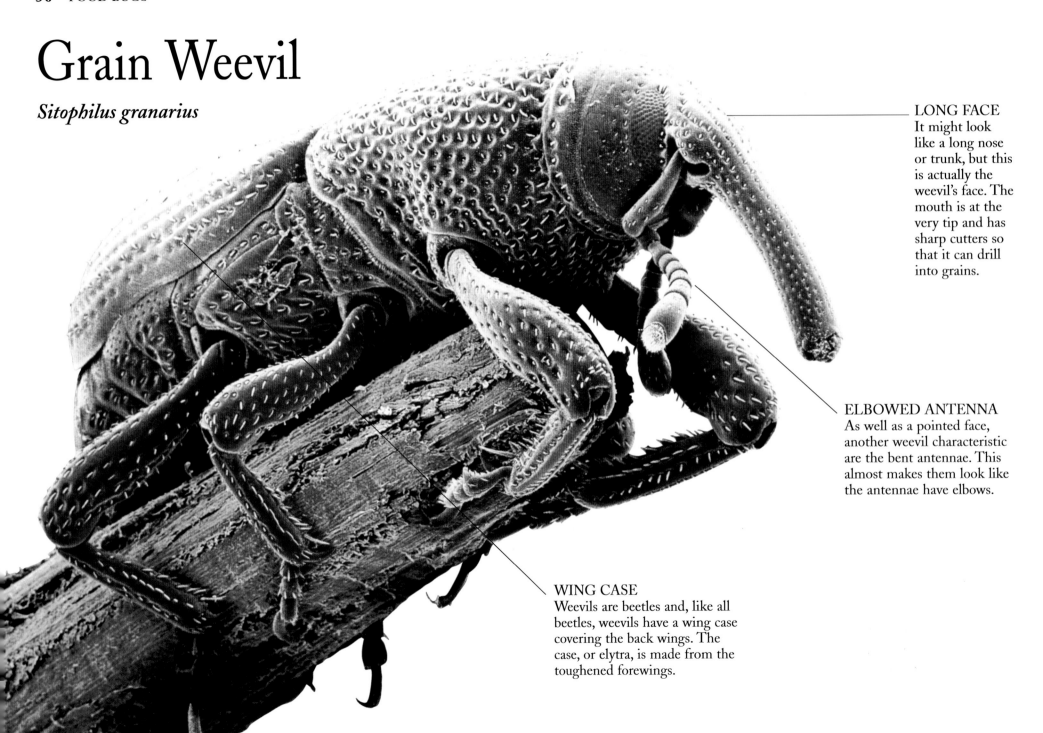

LONG FACE
It might look like a long nose or trunk, but this is actually the weevil's face. The mouth is at the very tip and has sharp cutters so that it can drill into grains.

ELBOWED ANTENNA
As well as a pointed face, another weevil characteristic are the bent antennae. This almost makes them look like the antennae have elbows.

WING CASE
Weevils are beetles and, like all beetles, weevils have a wing case covering the back wings. The case, or elytra, is made from the toughened forewings.

In the wild, weevils survive on nuts and seeds, so a farmer's grain harvest offers a ready-made food supply. (Grains are the seeds of wheat, rye, and barley—all types of grass.) Weevils drill holes through the outer skin of the grain to get at the soft germ inside. The grains are also the food supply for the weevils' grubs. The female weevil makes a hole in a grain and then turns around to place one egg inside it, using her egg-laying tube. She plugs the hole with sticky goo. Once they hatch, the grubs hollow out their grain. In less than a year, a gang of 100 weevils could have destroyed six million wheat grains!

Full point
(Magnified 4 times)

Grain weevil
(Magnified 4 times)

SIZE COMPARISON

▶ GRAIN WEEVILS SPEND their early life hidden inside a kernel. Only once they have turned into an adult do they bite their way outside.

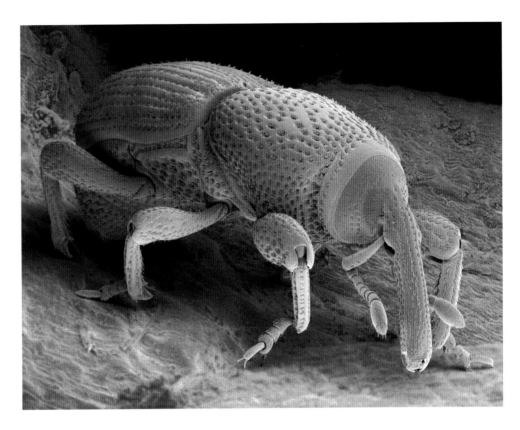

Cereal Destroyer

Grain weevils attack all types of cereal grains. They have even been known to live in stores of pasta, which is made from wheat. Once a grain store has been infected, there is not much you can do, except throw it all away and start again. Some granaries are sprayed with chemicals to make them smell bad to the weevils.

Did you know?

• Grain weevils have been a problem for a long time. The remains of weevils have been found in the ruins of Roman granaries built 2,000 years ago.

• Grains containing weevil grubs float. Unaffected grain sinks in water.

Ham Beetle

Necrobia ruficollis

ANTENNAE
The club-shaped antennae are sensitive to the chemicals given off by other animals—even after they are dead.

HAIRY BACK
Ham beetles have short hairs growing out of their backs. They are thickest on the toughened wing cases.

MOUTH
Most of the ham beetles' close relatives are hunters, and so the mouthparts are well built for cutting up dead bodies.

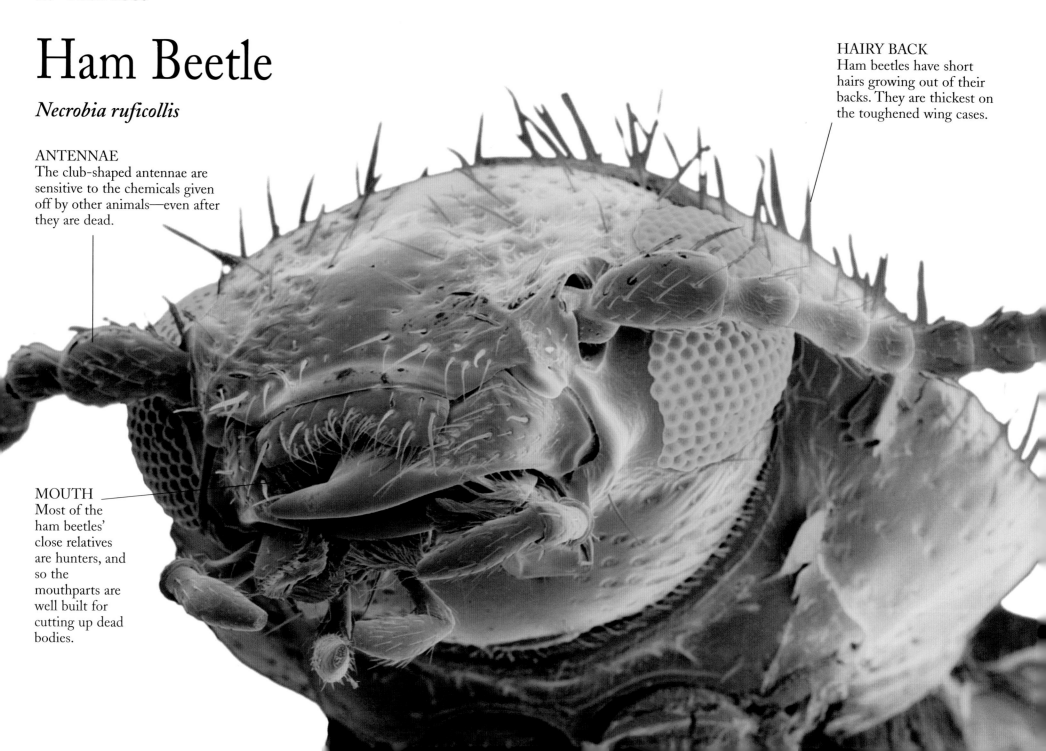

Ham beetles do not like fresh meat but prefer flesh that has dried out into fatty strings. In the wild, that means ham beetles are often found on the skin and bones left behind when bigger meat-eaters have eaten their fill. However, the finest hams are made by letting meat dry out for several weeks. That makes them perfect for ham beetles, which also like dried fish and salami. The adults nibble at the edges, but their grubs burrow deep into the food, looking for a rich seam of fat. Ham beetles are also found on dead bodies, which tells police experts the body has been lying undiscovered for a few months.

Full point
(Magnified 2 times)

Ham beetle
(Magnified 2 times)

SIZE COMPARISON

▶ THERE ARE TWO types of ham beetle. The worst pest has red legs. Black-legged ham beetles are not as much of a problem.

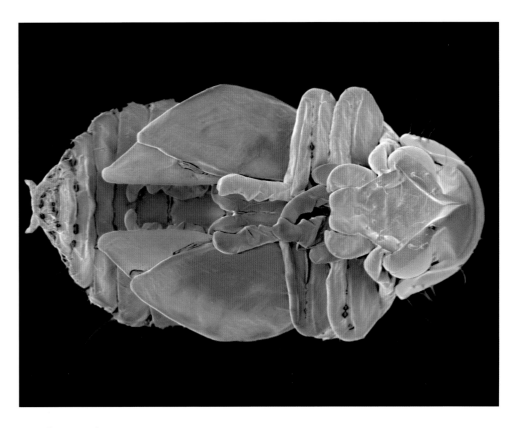

Ham Beetles and Egyptian Mummies

The remains of ham beetles have been found on the mummified bodies of Egyptian kings and queens. The presence of these beetles tell experts about what Egypt was like all those years ago. Today most of Egypt is a desert, with only a few patches of forest. But the ham beetles would have preferred a wetter kind of world, which means that ancient Egypt cannot have been as dry as the country is today.

Did you know?

• Ham beetles also end up in shipments of dried figs and other fruits.

• Relatives of ham beetles are useful hunters. They are utilized to kill off pests in timber yards.

• Adult ham beetles can live for more than a year and will feed on their own eggs if they have to do so.

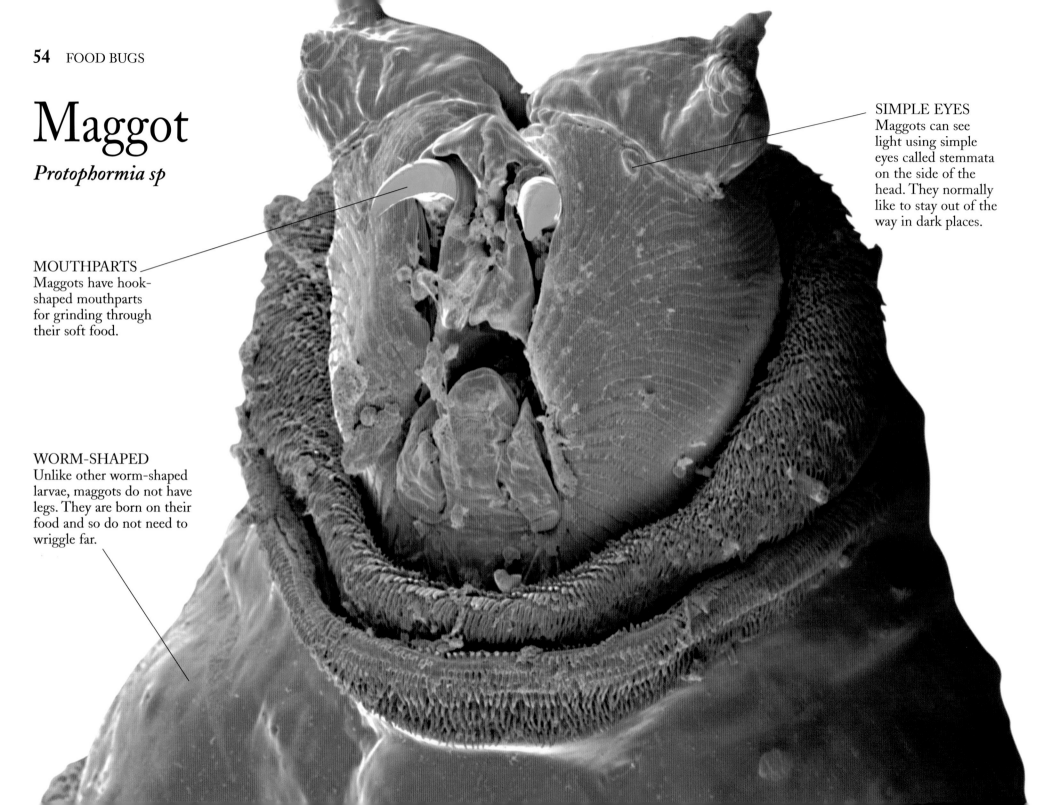

Maggot
Protophormia sp

MOUTHPARTS
Maggots have hook-shaped mouthparts for grinding through their soft food.

WORM-SHAPED
Unlike other worm-shaped larvae, maggots do not have legs. They are born on their food and so do not need to wriggle far.

SIMPLE EYES
Maggots can see light using simple eyes called stemmata on the side of the head. They normally like to stay out of the way in dark places.

No one likes finding something alive in their food, and there is perhaps nothing more disgusting than seeing a maggot wriggling around the kitchen. Fortunately our food is very clean and will be fine if it is stored properly. A maggot looks like a small worm but it is, in fact, a baby fly. Its mother laid its egg—looking like a tiny grain of rice—on a piece of food, ready for the maggot to eat. Each type of fly looks for different foods. Some want raw meat, others like fruits and vegetables. Whatever the meal, the maggots are hungry. They eat several times their own body weight each day.

Full point
(Magnified 2 times)

Maggot
(Magnified 2 times)

SIZE COMPARISON

▶ MAGGOTS AND SOME caterpillars live inside apples. Most affected apples rot quickly and fall off the tree early, so they are rarely picked and sent to the stores.

Cleaning Wounds

Maggots may seem dirty, but doctors use them to clean deep wounds so that they heal faster. The maggots are thoroughly washed to ensure they do not produce an infection and are then released into the cut. They wriggle around, munching on the dead tissue—and leave the healthy flesh to heal. The maggots bring their own medicine. Their saliva contains chemicals that kill bacteria.

Did you know?

• Maggots have two dark spots on their rear end. They look like eyes but are breathing holes, so the maggot can breathe with its head buried in food.

• Botfly maggots bury themselves in human skin. The bulge they make looks like a sore pimple. When it bursts, the fattened maggot slithers out!

• Maggots that are used as fishing bait can be dyed in several different colors to attract various kinds of fish.

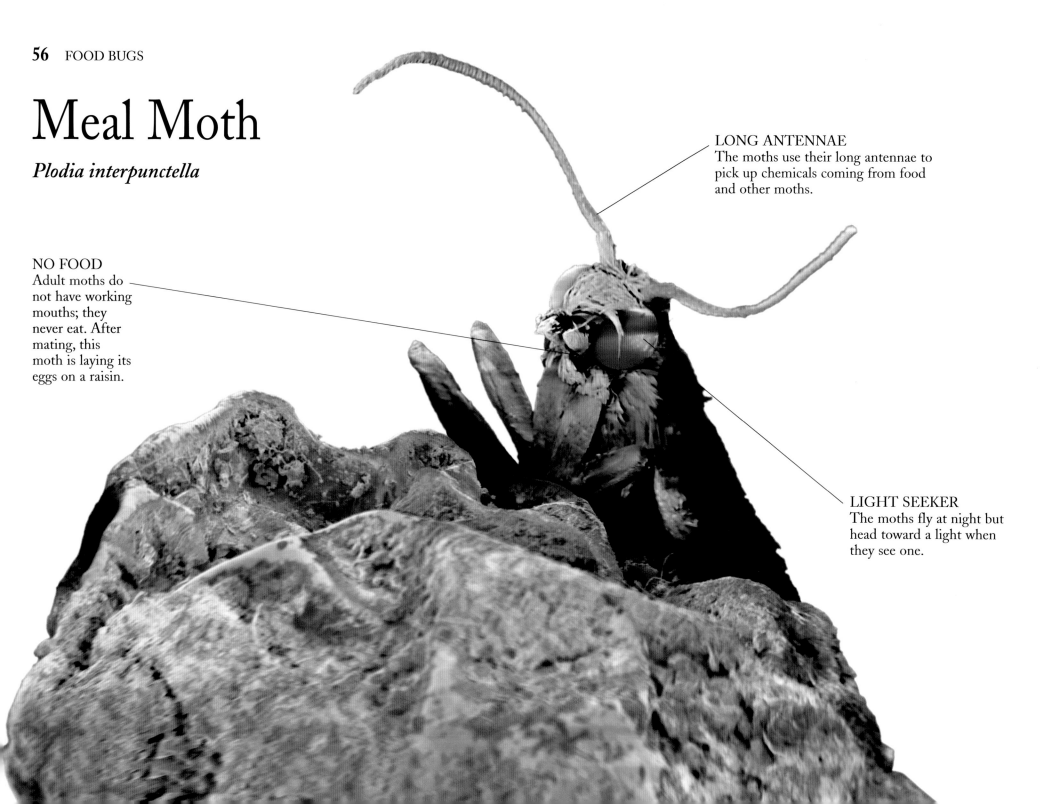

Meal Moth

Plodia interpunctella

LONG ANTENNAE
The moths use their long antennae to pick up chemicals coming from food and other moths.

NO FOOD
Adult moths do not have working mouths; they never eat. After mating, this moth is laying its eggs on a raisin.

LIGHT SEEKER
The moths fly at night but head toward a light when they see one.

Meal moths eat maize, wheat, and other cereal grains. They also live in the flour, or meal, made by milling grain. The worst pest is the Indian meal moth. However, this insect is from America, not India. It is named after it favorite food: cornmeal. When the pest was named in the 1850s, cornmeal was a common food eaten by Native American people, and was known then as Indian meal. Meal moths can ruin stores of grain and flour. The little white caterpillars do the damage, and also infest dried fruits and bread. When fully grown, the caterpillars hang their silky cocoons from the ceiling.

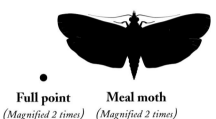

Full point	**Meal moth**
(Magnified 2 times)	*(Magnified 2 times)*

SIZE COMPARISON

▶ THE CATERPILLARS OF meal moths are called waxworms. They are very tough and are not killed off by cold weather. They just grow more slowly in chilly places, taking several months to grow into an adult moth.

Trapping Moths

Male moths are attracted to the pheromone smells produced by a female ready to mate. But they may be being fooled. Glue-filled moth traps are scented with the same smell as the female moths. The males race over to traps and meet a sticky end.

Did you know?

• People put a few bay leaves in their flour to fend off moths. The leaves smell horrible to the pests.

• Large granaries are fitted with drying fans that stop the stored grains from getting too damp. The moths find it harder to feed on dry grains.

Mealybug

Planococcus sp

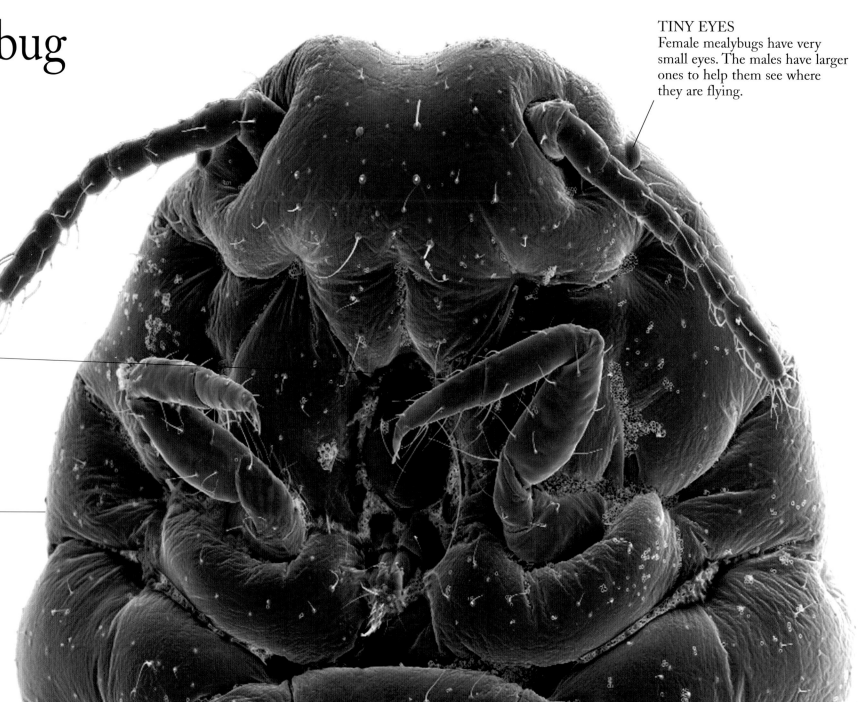

TINY EYES
Female mealybugs have very small eyes. The males have larger ones to help them see where they are flying.

FEEDING SPIKE
Female mealybugs suck up sap through a narrow pipe called a stylet. When it is not feeding, the long tube is stored inside a protective tube.

SOFT BODY
Mealybugs are so tiny they do not have thickened skins like many insects. They cover their body in wax instead.

Mealybugs never eat but only drink the sap of plants. They attack many food plants, such as lemon trees, grape vines, and sugarcane. A swarm of bugs can take so much sap that a plant's leaves dry out and fall off. Mealybugs do not even need to suck. Sap is pumped through the plant, and once a bug has tapped into it using its long feeding tube, the sap is forced down its throat. The life of a male and female mealybug could not be more different. The females do not grow wings and do little but feed. The males do grow wings and fly off to find mates—but without a mouth they do not live for long.

Full point
(Magnified 8 times)

Mealybug
(Magnified 8 times)

SIZE COMPARISON

▶ MEALYBUGS DO NOT eat meal or flour, but they look like they are covered in it. The white dust is actually fluffy wax. The wax protects the bugs from attacks by tiny wasps that want to lay their eggs on top of them.

Ants and Mealybugs

Their food is so watery that mealybugs produce an almost constant trickle of liquid waste. This urine is known as honeydew because it is actually quite sweet. Ants guard flocks of mealybugs and "milk" them for the honeydew, which the ants love to drink. Honeybees also collect the liquid, which is similar to nectar to make honey. Honeydew honey is very dark and said to be very healthy.

Did you know?

• Some mealy bugs do not lay eggs. The tiny nymphs grow inside the mother and she gives birth to them.

• A species of ladybug is known as the mealybug destroyer. The beetle's grubs have the same fluffy look as the bugs. This disguise lets the destroyers get in among their prey unnoticed.

Rosemary Beetle

Chrysolina americana

SMALL WINGS
Rosemary beetles cannot fly, even as adults. Like most beetles, they have a pair of wings underneath the hinged dome of wing cases on the back. However, the wings are too small to get the beetle off the ground.

METALLIC STRIPES
The beetles have shiny bodies with green and purple stripes running along the side and back.

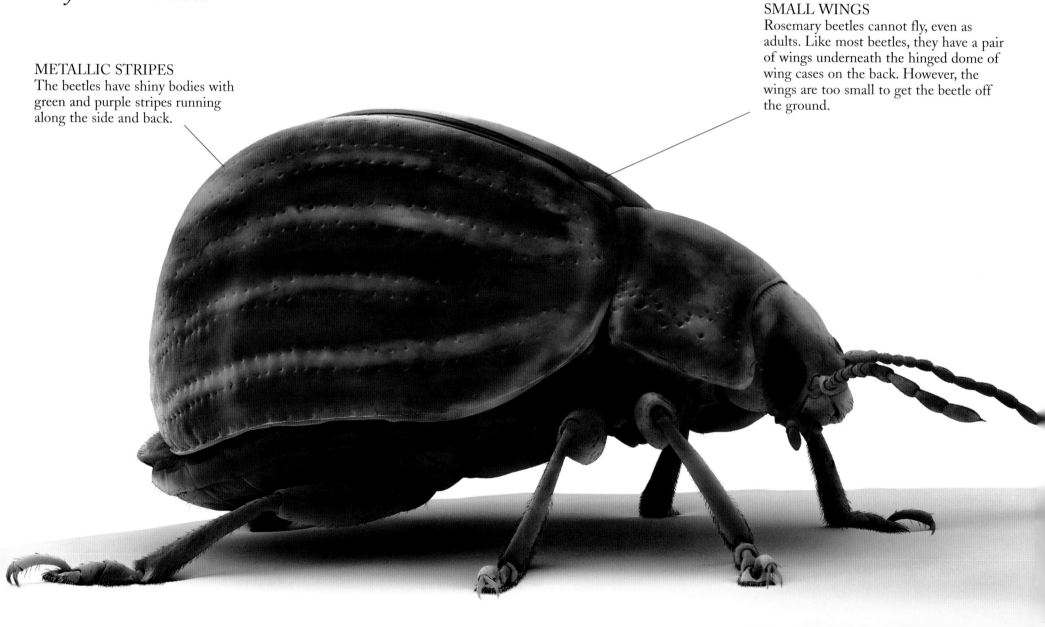

Rosemary beetles love herbs. In fact, they eat nothing else. This beetle comes from southern Europe, where it feasts on lavender and rosemary. In recent years, it has moved north and now eats other herbs, such as thyme, mint, and sage. Being from the warm south, rosemary beetles do not cram their whole life cycle into the warm summer like many insects. They lie dormant for most of the summer, waking up to feed and mate only in August. The females lay their eggs under leaves and graze on the herbs through the winter—when it is not too cold. The eggs hatch in spring, becoming adults within two months.

Full point
(Magnified 3 times)

Rosemary beetle
(Magnified 3 times)

SIZE COMPARISON

▶ THE BEETLE'S PLUMP larva, or grub, clings to herb leaves with its six legs. It feeds for a few weeks before dropping to the ground and then buries itself before pupating into an adult.

Evidence of Climate Change

Rosemary beetles have recently invaded Britain. They were first spotted in Surrey, in southeastern England, in 1994 and have since moved to other parts of Britain. No one knows how far they will spread. The beetles feed most of the year, so a cold winter may kill many of them off. However, the beetle's arrival may be a sign that climate change is making Britain warmer.

Did you know?

• The scientific name for the rosemary beetle is *Chrysolina americana*. But the beetle is a European species, not American.

• Gardeners find it difficult to get rid of rosemary beetles. If they want to eat the herbs that the beetles are attacking, they must avoid spraying them with chemicals.

In the Backyard

IMAGINE WHAT A BACKYARD WOULD LOOK LIKE if you were just $\frac{1}{5}$ in (5mm) tall. A lawn would be a thick jungle of grass. A patio would be a desert of rocks with a few oases of weeds and moss. In the distance immense flowers tower above the countryside like colorful skyscrapers. But watch out, this miniature world is fraught with danger and there are monsters everywhere. Vicious wasps circle overhead, while bloodthirsty centipedes could tunnel out from underneath you at any second.

But there are some great sights to see. Butterflies flit in the sunlight as ants lounge on a tree trunk minding a herd of aphids. Stand back, here comes a slug. It will leave you well alone but get out of the way while it slides slowly by. Backyards and gardens are meant to be enjoyed but you won't have enjoyed it quite like this before. Find out about a secret force of minute wasps that start out life inside the bodies of other micromonsters—and have to eat their way out! Other backyard monsters are less interested in staying out of sight. Cicadas bang out some of the loudest calls in the animal kingdom. A walk through your backyard will never be the same again.

Ant

Formica sp

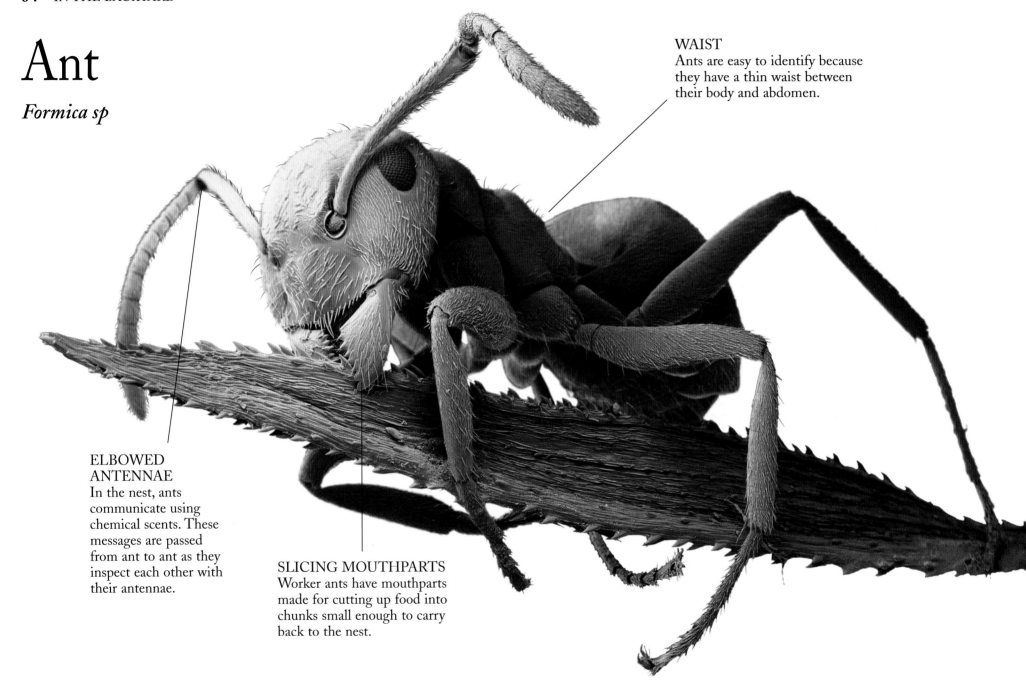

WAIST
Ants are easy to identify because they have a thin waist between their body and abdomen.

ELBOWED ANTENNAE
In the nest, ants communicate using chemical scents. These messages are passed from ant to ant as they inspect each other with their antennae.

SLICING MOUTHPARTS
Worker ants have mouthparts made for cutting up food into chunks small enough to carry back to the nest.

Most ants' nests are hidden, but it's easy enough to see ants at work. These wingless insects live in large groups, all working for the mother—the queen ant—who stays home producing eggs. All the ants are her daughters, and they maintain the nest and feed their younger sisters. The ants you can see are the older females collecting plant and animal food. The queen also produces a few sons each summer, and new queens. These ants have wings, and they swarm out of the nest together, creating a short-lived swarm. They mate, and the young queens then look for a place to build a new nest.

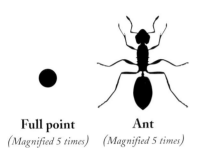

Full point
(Magnified 5 times)

Ant
(Magnified 5 times)

SIZE COMPARISON

▶ TINY ARGENTINE ANTS live in mind-bogglingly huge supercolonies—or groups of colonies. One supercolony runs for 3,725 miles (6,000km) along the European coast and contains billions of ants. Each ant does not belong to a single nest but is welcomed into any nest in the supercolony.

Locked-on

Flatworms infect ants and use the insects to get inside an even bigger animal. The infected ant's jaws lock when it is biting into food, and it gets stuck on a blade of grass or leaf. When a cow or sheep comes along, it swallows the paralyzed ant along with its food, and the flatworm has reached its new home.

Did you know?

• Army ants live in warm parts of the world. They do not have a nest, but are always on the march in long columns. When it is time to rest, the ants form into a ball of bodies around the queen.

• Honeypot ant workers store sweet liquid food inside their bodies and feed it to the rest of the colony. The storer ants swell up so much that they cannot walk.

Aphid

Aphidoidea

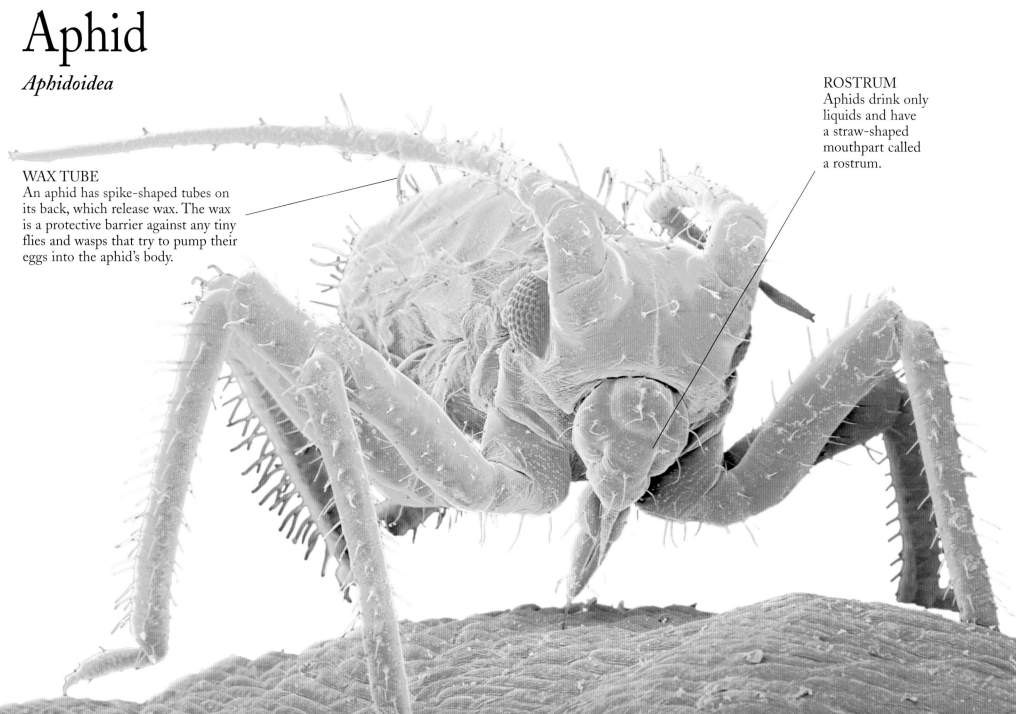

WAX TUBE
An aphid has spike-shaped tubes on its back, which release wax. The wax is a protective barrier against any tiny flies and wasps that try to pump their eggs into the aphid's body.

ROSTRUM
Aphids drink only liquids and have a straw-shaped mouthpart called a rostrum.

Aphids are also known as greenflies. But they are not flies and most are not green. They are insects that live on flowers and other garden plants, sucking out their sap. As any gardener knows, aphids are a pest. Aphid mothers do not need a male to produce young. They give birth to clones—tiny versions of themselves—which cover the plant. Aphids drain the liquid from a delicate flower, and their sweet waste produces dark mold stains that spoil colorful blooms. When winter approaches, females begin to produce both sons and daughters. These mate and lay eggs that hatch in spring.

Full point
(Magnified 10 times)

Aphid
(Magnified 10 times)

SIZE COMPARISON

▶ APHIDS GIVE BIRTH to several generations of wingless nymphs until the plant becomes overcrowded. Then winged daughters are produced, which fly off to find a new plant to attack.

Too Busy for Defense

Aphids are so busy feeding that they cannot defend themselves. Large herds of aphids are protected by a force of tough soldiers. For example, the soldiers of bamboo aphids are armed with a sharp horn on their heads. The soldiers do not reproduce and spend their time fighting off attacking insects and cleaning any parasites from the breeding aphids.

Did you know?

• Dairy ants collect aphid eggs and store them in their nest in winter. In spring, the ants put the eggs on a plant. Once the aphids have hatched, the ants come back and drink the aphids' honeydew—their sweet-tasting liquid waste.

• Aphids spread many plant diseases that can ruin entire fields of crops, such as sugarcane and cabbages.

Butterfly

Lepidoptera

EYE
Butterflies can see ultraviolet light, which is invisible to us. Flowers look very different in UV and often show very clearly where an insect can find the nectar.

COILED UP
A butterfly's tube-shaped proboscis may be as long as its body. When it is not being used, it is coiled up safely under the head.

Butterflies are some of the largest and certainly most colorful insects to visit your backyard. Despite their large wings, butterflies are only average flyers and slowly flutter past in a haphazard way. Butterflies eat sweet liquids—mainly the nectar in flowers—but also the ooze from fallen fruits and even liquid seeping from dung. Most people welcome the arrival of butterflies in summer and gardeners often plant flowers especially for them, but few are glad to see the caterpillars that hatch from their eggs. Most caterpillars are pests and will eat holes through the leaves of many garden plants.

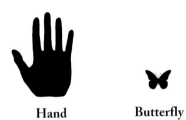

Hand   **Butterfly**

SIZE COMPARISON

▶ BUTTERFLIES LIKE FLOWERS that give them a wide platform to land on. To get at the nectar, they must push past the pollen, which sticks to their bodies. The butterflies carry the pollen to the next flower, where the plant uses it to produce seeds.

Butterflies and Moths

The biggest difference between butterflies and moths is that butterflies come out during the day and most moths are seen at night. Experts think that the two groups evolved in response to bats. The first bats appeared about 55 million years ago and fed mainly on night-flying moths. Some species of moth began to fly during daylight to avoid the bats, and these evolved into today's butterflies.

Did you know?

• Butterflies do not get much salt from nectar drinks, so they like to suck salt from rocks—or even from your sweat.

• Bright colors warn birds and other predators that these butterflies are poisonous—but for many butterflies the bright colors are just a disguise.

Centipede

Lithobius

FEELING THE WAY
Few centipedes can see very well. Most have no eyes at all and must feel their way with their long antennae.

LEG PAIR
Centipedes have one pair of legs growing from each body segment. Garden centipedes have about 30 legs.

KILLER CLAWS
Centipedes kill with a hug, not a bite. The first pair of legs are not used for walking. They work like pincers, spearing prey with their poisoned claws.

Centipedes have no enemies, but seek out slugs, worms, insects, and spiders in the undergrowth and beneath rocks. Few of their prey can outrun a centipede. And victims are quickly put to death by a poison that drools from killer claws. The word centipede means "one hundred feet," but most have less than 40 legs, although some long species have more than 300! So many legs is a sign that centipedes are not close relatives of insects or spiders. They are myriapods (many-legged animals), which were were among the first creatures to live on land—and centipedes were the first hunters.

Full point
(100%)

Centipede
(100%)

SIZE COMPARISON

▶ CENTIPEDES ALSO hunt inside people's homes. House centipedes often have very long legs, which has earned them the nickname of mustache bug. They are one of the insects that will take on a house spider.

Coordinating the Legs

Centipedes must scuttle along quickly to chase down their prey. With all legs pumping, centipedes can travel more than 3ft (1m) in about 3 seconds. But how do they stop themselves from tripping up on all those legs? The legs at the front of the body are shorter than the ones further back. As they dash along, the back legs are long enough to step over the front ones, so there is never a clash.

Did you know?

• The world's largest centipedes are 12in (30cm) long. They live in warm parts of the world. A bite from one will not kill you, but you will feel unwell for a few hours.

• Centipedes fend off attacking ants by squirting them with glue, which sticks the insects together.

Cicada

Cicadoidea

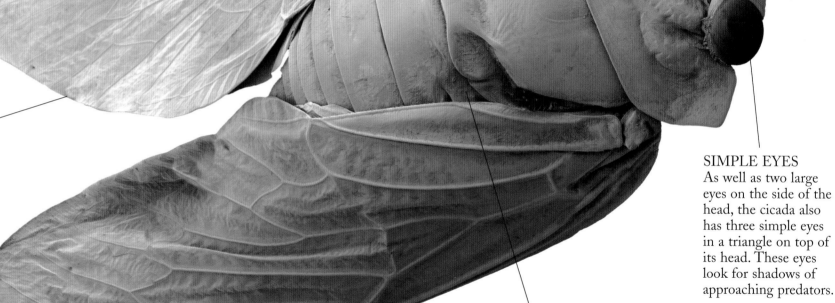

WINGS
Cicadas have four see-through wings with thick veins. The hind pair is smaller than the front wings and are normally tucked underneath.

SIMPLE EYES
As well as two large eyes on the side of the head, the cicada also has three simple eyes in a triangle on top of its head. These eyes look for shadows of approaching predators.

TYMBALS
The cicada makes sound using two drumlike sections called tymbals on its abdomen, which click when they are pulled by a muscle. A tymbal can produce hundreds of clicks in just one second.

If there are cicadas in your neighborhood, you will know about it: They are the loudest insects on Earth. Cicadas live in warm parts of the world. They spend most of their lives as wingless nymphs that suck the juice from plant roots buried underground. The nymphs stay hidden away for a long time—the world's longest-living insect is a type of cicada that survives for 17 years! The buried nymphs are very quiet. They make noise only once they have crawled up a tree trunk and changed into an adult. Only male cicadas produce the loud, rattling calls to attract females. Each species has its own song.

Full point
(Magnified 3 times)

Cicada
(Magnified 3 times)

SIZE COMPARISON

▶ CICADA NYMPHS ARE built for life underground—they have forefeet that look like pincers for digging. When fully developed, the nymph climbs a tree trunk and its back splits open to reveal an adult inside. The adult's wings are squashed at first, but they straighten out as blood pumps into them.

Paralyzing Cicadas

Cicada-killer wasps turn cicadas into zombies and then let their larvae eat them alive. The large female wasps paralyze the cicada with a sting, and then haul the large insects into a burrow and lay an egg on it. The wasp mothers stock a male egg with one cicada but larger females get two or three.

Did you know?

• In Southeast Asia, cicadas are a tasty food. They are served as kabobs or are meaty ingredients for a stir-fry.

• Cicadas living in deserts keep cool by letting plant sap trickle from holes in their skin. They are one of the very few insects to sweat like us.

Dung Fly

Scatophaga stercoraria

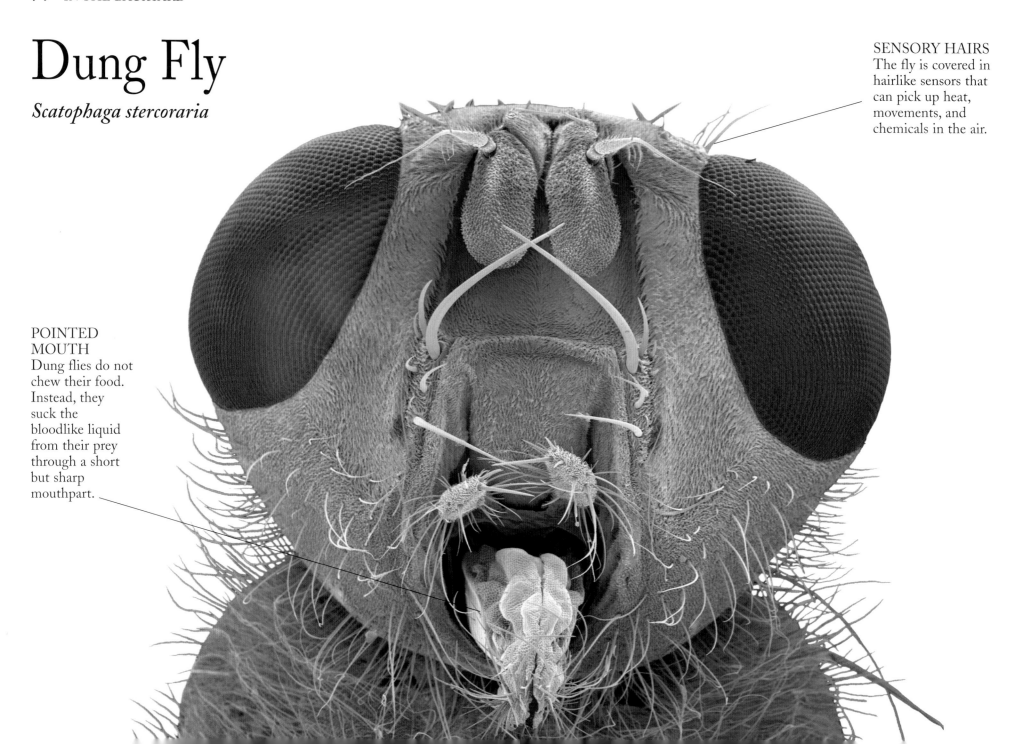

SENSORY HAIRS
The fly is covered in hairlike sensors that can pick up heat, movements, and chemicals in the air.

POINTED MOUTH
Dung flies do not chew their food. Instead, they suck the bloodlike liquid from their prey through a short but sharp mouthpart.

As their name suggests, dung flies do look for soft cow pies and fresh horse manure for their maggots, but they will also lay their eggs on fallen fruits and rotting leaves. Adult female flies sometimes nibble on the dung before laying their eggs, but the males are hunters. Their favorite victims are other flies: They often prey upon blow flies, which are also attracted to dung. Dung flies lay their eggs carefully so they do not sink and drown in the sloppiest parts. Many dung-fly maggots do not just eat the dung itself but prey on the other types of maggots that are munching their way through it.

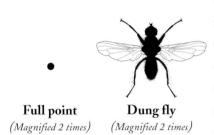

Full point
(*Magnified 2 times*)

Dung fly
(*Magnified 2 times*)

SIZE COMPARISON

▶ ADULT DUNG FLIES may sip a little nectar from time to time, but they also visit plants for more deadly reasons. They sit on flowers and leaves looking harmless, but when another fly or aphid arrives to feed, the dung fly will go in for the kill.

Robber Flies

Dung flies fall prey to even tougher insects called robber flies. These large flies have long legs, which they use to snatch dung flies straight out of the air. Robber flies do not travel alone, though. Tiny flies just ¹⁄₂₅in (1mm) long hitch a ride. While the robber fly is drinking its victim's blood, these little passengers drink up any droplets that dribble out.

Did you know?

• Male dung flies look golden, but the females are more greenish.

• Some dung flies lay their eggs on slimy seaweed washed up on the shore.

• Several dung fly maggots do not eat dung at all. They tunnel their way through plant stems and fleshy leaves.

Earthworm

Lumbricus terrestris

HOOKED HAIRS
Bristly hairs stick out from the side
of the body, helping the worm to grip
the soil as it wriggles along.

BODY SEGMENTS
Worm bodies are made
up of dozens of
repeating segments.

You are most likely to see earthworms after a shower of heavy rain. Usually, they avoid coming to the surface, where they make easy prey for birds. Also, they die when exposed to strong sunlight for too long. When it rains, though, the worms have to come to the surface to avoid being drowned. The rest of the time, the worms are eating their way through the ground. They eat the soil—sand and all—and digest any food mixed into it. The tunnels they create act as airways through the soil. Plant roots need to take in air just like all living things, so the worms keep the plants in garden growing.

Hand **Earthworm**

SIZE COMPARISON

▶ THE THICK SECTION about a third of the way down the earthworm is called the saddle, or clitellum. This is where the worm makes its babies. The babies grow from slimy cocoons that develop on the side of the saddle and then fall off.

Worm Charmers

Earthworms are a useful fishing bait, but digging them up can be a long and tiring business. Worm charmers can bring the earthworms to the surface for collection. The charmers use a number of methods to send thumping vibrations through soil. The worms rush to the surface. Experts say that the sounds make the worms believe a mole is coming to eat them.

Did you know?

• The longest earthworms come from Australia. They grow to 13ft (4m) long!

• The world record for worm charming is held by a 10-year-old girl, who collected 567 worms during the World Championships held in 2009.

• An earthworm has five hearts, all in the front part of the body. Cutting it in half will not make two new worms, just one dead one.

Honeybee

Apis mellifera

HAIRY COAT
Bees fly even when it is too cold for most insects. Heat from the strong flight muscles warms up the body, and it stays warm thanks to a covering of hairs.

TASTE TESTERS
The bee tastes her way through the flower and hive using chemical sensors on the antennae.

NO RED EYE
Honeybees cannot see the color red. They normally head for yellow and purple flowers.

The hive of the honeybee is ruled by a single queen. Only she produces young, and all the worker bees are her daughters. Younger workers stay at home, caring for the larvae and building the honeycomb. Older bees forage—collect nectar and pollen from flowers. Nectar is carried in the forager bee's honey stomach, a pouch in her throat. The pollen is packed into comb-shaped baskets on the back legs. Bees transfer pollen grains between flowers, enabling the plants to make seeds. As well as helping garden flowers, honeybees pollinate billions of dollars worth of fruits and vegetables each year.

Full point **Honeybee**
(Magnified 2 times) *(Magnified 2 times)*

SIZE COMPARISON

▶ HONEYBEES STING ONLY if they must. Each bee can sting only once because the sharp stinger gets stuck in your skin. The bee cannot fly away without ripping open its abdomen. That is enough to kill it—but if the sting protects the rest of the hive, the bee will have died for a good reason.

Manufacturing Honey

Honeybees manufacture honey as a food store to keep the hive going during the winter—and to feed to larvae. Honey starts out as nectar, which is emptied into the honeycomb by foraging bees. Other workers then fan the liquid with their wings. This drives away the water, leaving a sticky and sweet gel.

Did you know?

• Beekeepers use smoke to stop bees from stinging them when they collect honey. The smoke tricks the bees into thinking that the hive is on fire, and so they dash inside to gulp down honey before it is too late.

• Killer bees are a cross between African and European honeybees. They were released by accident in Brazil in the 1950s.

• Male bees, or drones, mate just once, and they do it with such force that their body explodes!

Hornet

Vespa crabro

BITING MOUTH
Hornets cut up their prey with powerful slicing mouthparts.

WINGS
Like all wasps (and bees), hornets have four wings, but the smaller back wings are hooked to the larger ones in front, so the four work just like two.

HANGING LEGS
Hornets and wasps fly with the legs on show. If you cannot see the legs, the insect is probably a bumblebee or maybe a moth with a wasp's coloring.

ornets may look tougher and uglier than smaller wasps, but hornets are pretty harmless. Their sting is no more painful than that of an ordinary yellowjacket wasp. And hornets are more likely to leave you alone. They won't spoil a picnic because they are not interested in sweet drinks and fruit: They eat meatier food and often prey on honeybees. Nevertheless, like many other wasps and bees, hornets can sting. They pump poison through a sharp spike on their rear end. And unlike honeybees, the hornet can use its sting many times over—which it will do if you try to pick one up!

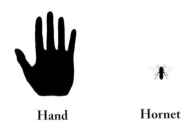

Hand   **Hornet**

SIZE COMPARISON

▶ THE GIANT ASIAN HORNET is the largest wasp in the world. It grows to five times the size of a common wasp and has a sting to match. Japanese people call it the Yak Killer. It cannot kill an animal as big as that, but the monster wasp's stinger poison is strong enough to kill a person if he or she is attacked many times at once.

The Deadly Hornet

In Japan, giant Asian hornets kill about 40 people every year—more victims than any other animal, even wild bears! The hornet is even more deadly to honeybees. Once one hornet finds a hive, it leaves a scent that attracts dozens of others. The bees do not stand a chance!

Did you know?

• A hornet nest will have just a few hundred insects. A wasp nest could have 10,000.

• People are so frightened of hornets that they destroy the nests as soon as they find one. Sadly, that means hornets may become extinct in some parts of Europe.

Hover fly

Syrphidae

ROUNDED EYES
Hover flies are related to bluebottles and houseflies and they have the same large rounded eyes, not the tear-shaped goggles of wasps.

STUBBY ANTENNAE
The hover fly has tiny antennae, unlike a wasp's flexible feelers.

FLOWER FOOD
Hover flies might like to look tough but they only sip nectar and nibble pollen with their small mouthparts.

Hover flies are the masters of disguise. It takes a sharp eye to see that the insects buzzing close to the flowerbed is not a stinging wasp or bee but actually a harmless fly. Hover flies are not even closely related to stinging bugs, but they have the same tell-tale black and yellow stripes. That is enough to warn predators, including birds, to stay away. Hover flies are sometimes called flower flies, for the adults feed mainly on nectar and pollen. The maggots, though, eat a range of food, including aphids, which cause a lot of damage to crops, and so hover flies are used to control these pests.

Full point	**Hover fly**
(100%)	*(100%)*

SIZE COMPARISON

▶ HOVER FLIES MAY fool people and many other animals into thinking they are a stinging wasp, but that will not help them if they land on a flower that is home to a crab spider. These spiders do not bother looking their prey up and down. If it smells right, they will attack.

Rat-Tailed Maggots

Some hover-fly maggots have a nasty nickname—rat-tailed maggots. These insects live in drains where the water is stagnant or stale. There is hardly any oxygen mixed into this water, so the maggots must take breaths of air. They stay connected to the air using a long, flexible snorkel that sticks out of their bottoms. This fleshy tail earns them their name.

Did you know?

• Some hover-fly maggots are fierce hunters that kill whole herds of greenfly.

• Rat-tailed maggots are good bait for ice fishing.

• Hover-fly maggots infest the bulbs of narcissus and daffodils, stopping the flowers from sprouting in spring.

Jumping Spider

Salticidae

TEARING FANGS
A jumping spider bites its victim as soon as it crash lands on top. The fangs then slice up the food.

BIG EYES
Jumping spiders have six eyes in all. The main pair are tubes that fill most of the head. They produce a clear picture of prey, even in dim light.

HELPING HAND
Flexible palps either side of the fangs help to push bits of food into the mouth.

Jumping spiders are the superheroes of the bug world, able to leap huge distances and to see far into the distance. They are only tiny, perhaps a few millimeters across, but they can leap 12in (30cm) in one bound. That is the equivalent of a person jumping the length of a soccer pitch, from one penalty area to the other! Jumping spiders live mainly in hot countries, where they use their powers to ambush ants and other insects. To hit their prey, the spiders need a very accurate targeting system. Most of this work is done by the front pair of eyes, which are so large that they take up more room in the head than the spider's brain!

Full point
(Magnified 2 times)

Jumping spider
(Magnified 2 times)

SIZE COMPARISON

▶ JUMPING SPIDERS DO NOT take unnecessary risks. They creep very carefully as close possible to their intended victim before jumping. They also tie on a silk safety line to stop them from falling too far.

Mating Display

Jumping spiders lurk out of sight when they are hunting. But to find a mate they become real show-offs. The males have brightly colored hairs on their fangs and front legs, which they wave like tiny flags. Some add to the display by curling up their abdomen to give an extra splash of color.

Did you know?

• Jumping spiders have hairy feet, which help them get a grip on smooth leaves— and struggling prey.

• Jumping spiders can see four primary colors: red, yellow, blue, and ultraviolet (which is invisible to us).

• One species of jumping spider lives on the high slopes of Mount Everest.

Lacewing

Chrysoperia carnea

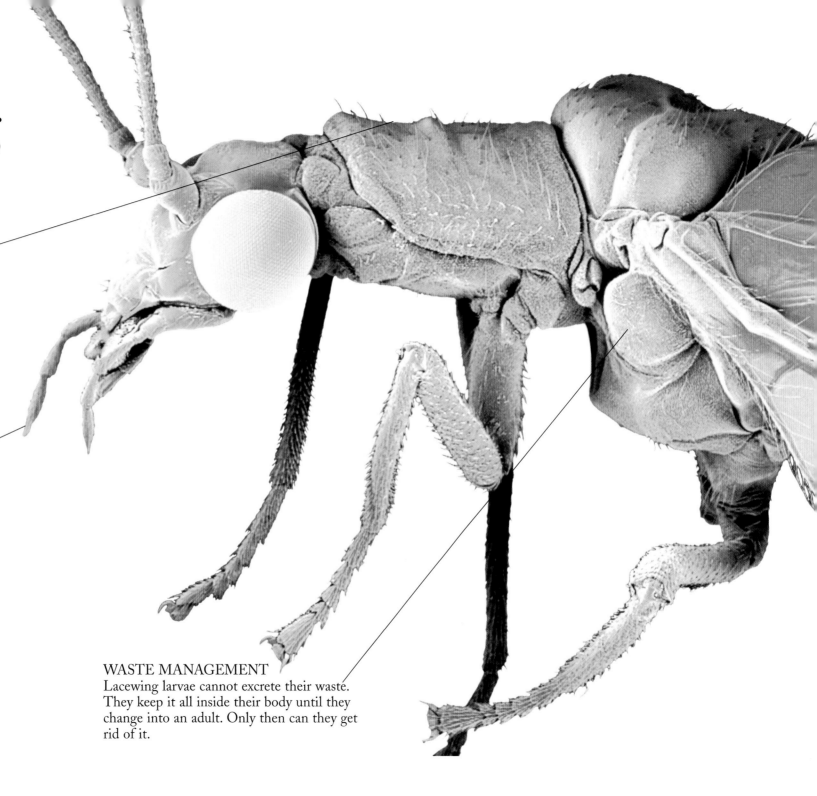

WINGS
Lacewings got their name from their large, see-through wings that are very delicate and are supported by a network of veins.

PINCER MOVEMENT
The hunter larva has pincer-shaped mouthparts that clasp prey while pumping in venom.

WASTE MANAGEMENT
Lacewing larvae cannot excrete their waste. They keep it all inside their body until they change into an adult. Only then can they get rid of it.

It is hard to imagine that a delicate green lacewing fluttering weakly between plants was once a skilled killer. But all lacewings start out as bloodthirsty larvae that can kill 300 aphids in a single day! Tiny larvae hatch from eggs laid on top of a stalk stuck to a leaf. The stalk stops other insects from reaching the egg but, once hatched, the baby lacewing does not need protection. Its powerful pincers spear small prey, killing them with venom, which also turns the dead animal into a meal of meaty mush for the larva to suck up. Once the larvae has become an adult, it will feast on nectar and other sweet liquids.

Full point
(100%)

Lacewing
(100%)

SIZE COMPARISON

▶ A LACEWING LARVA will camouflage itself by weaving bits of moss, bark, and even its dead victims into the hairs on its back.

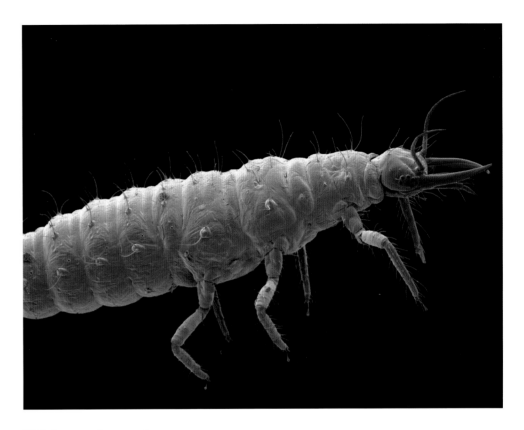

Mating Signals

Lacewings send secret love songs to each other. The insect shakes its body to send vibrations through the twig or shoot it is standing on. A predator cannot tell where this message is coming from, but another lacewing on the same plant will know that a possible mate is close.

Did you know?

• Beaded lacewing larvae have a special way of catching prey—they fart at them. The blast of gas is enough to stun the victim just long enough for the lacewing to bite it to death.

• Adult lacewings have ears on their wings, which can pick up the high-pitched calls of a bat before the winged hunter swoops in to eat them.

Ladybug

Coccinella septempunctata

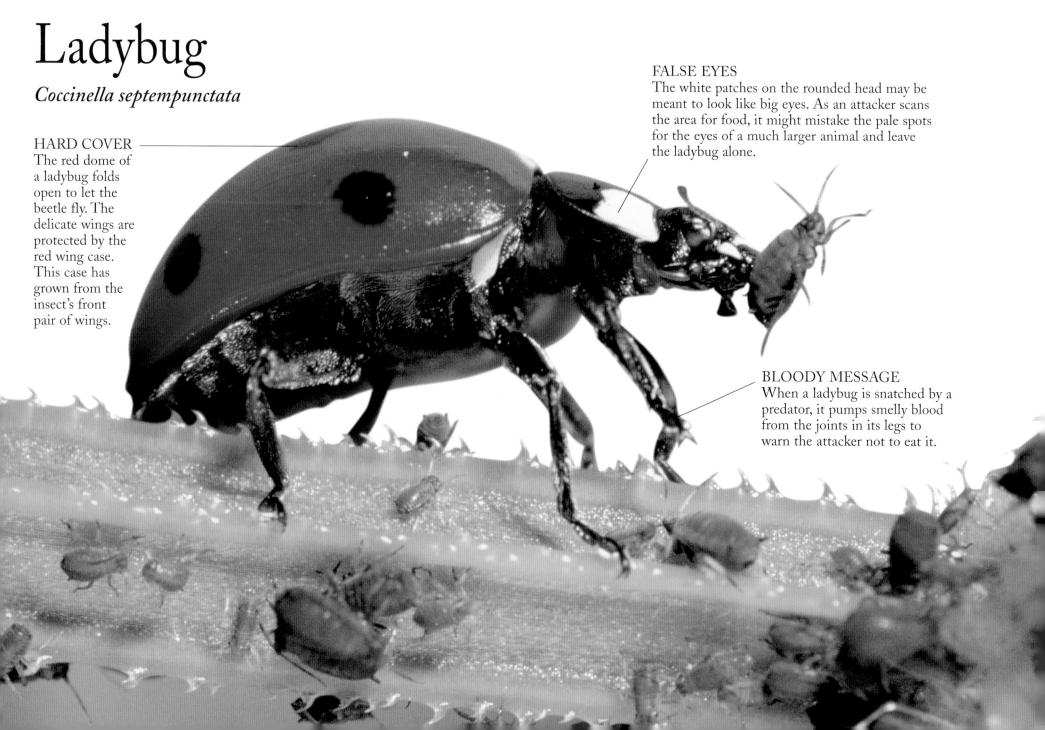

HARD COVER
The red dome of a ladybug folds open to let the beetle fly. The delicate wings are protected by the red wing case. This case has grown from the insect's front pair of wings.

FALSE EYES
The white patches on the rounded head may be meant to look like big eyes. As an attacker scans the area for food, it might mistake the pale spots for the eyes of a much larger animal and leave the ladybug alone.

BLOODY MESSAGE
When a ladybug is snatched by a predator, it pumps smelly blood from the joints in its legs to warn the attacker not to eat it.

Ladybugs, or ladybirds, are one of the most familiar backyard insects. Their bright red beetle bodies make them easy to spot. Ladybugs are not afraid to show themselves. We can see them easily, and so can hungry birds, but the bright, spotted body is a clear signal to predators to stay away. Ladybugs taste very bad. A young bird may eat a ladybug once, but the experience will teach it to avoid anything else that looks the same. This leaves ladybugs free to go hunting themselves. Both the larvae and the adults are aphid eaters. An adult ladybug could get through 1,000 aphids in one day!

• **Full point**
(*Magnified 2 times*)

Ladybird
(*Magnified 2 times*)

SIZE COMPARISON

▶ YOUNG LADYBUGS LOOK a lot less cute than the adults. They are streamlined killing machines. They hunt and eat constantly for three weeks, before changing into an adult. Like their parents, the larvae taste bad and have bitter chemicals stored in studs along the back.

Religious Connection

Ladybugs are named after the Virgin Mary, the mother of Jesus Christ. She is often referred to simply as "Our Lady." Centuries ago, people believed that Mary sent the bright ladybugs from heaven to fight off the insects that were destroying their crops. More than once, an army of ladybugs has helped to save crops and prevent people from starving.

Did you know?

• To the Irish, ladybugs are known as "God's little cow," while Iranians know them as "cobblers."

• Farmers are happy to see ladybugs, except if they are growing grapes. If ladybugs get mixed into the harvested grapes, they will make the wine taste bitter.

• Ladybugs come into houses in winter, looking for a warm place to shelter.

Long Horned Beetle

Cerambycidae

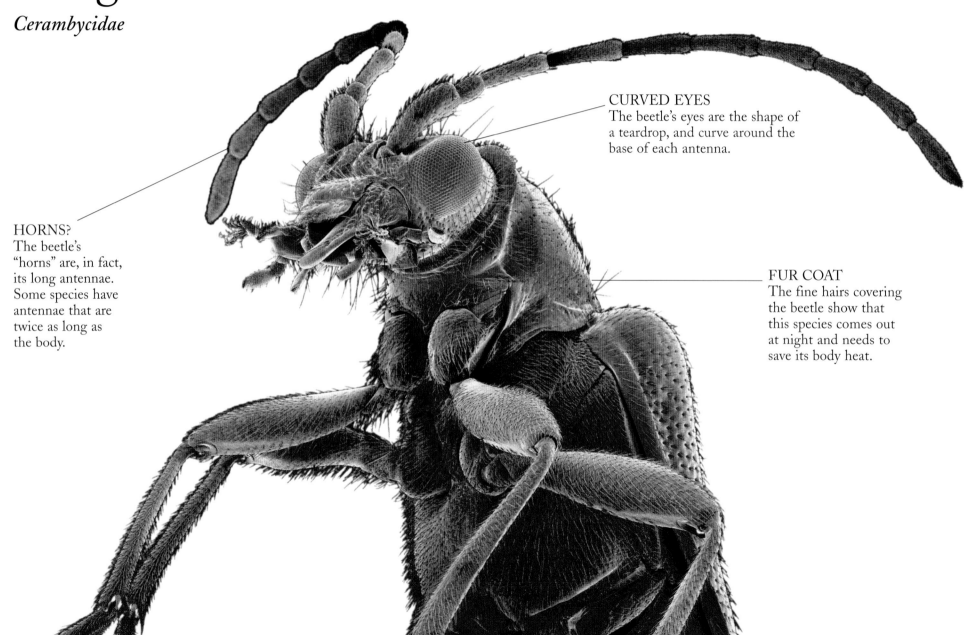

CURVED EYES
The beetle's eyes are the shape of
a teardrop, and curve around the
base of each antenna.

HORNS?
The beetle's
"horns" are, in fact,
its long antennae.
Some species have
antennae that are
twice as long as
the body.

FUR COAT
The fine hairs covering
the beetle show that
this species comes out
at night and needs to
save its body heat.

Long horned beetles live all over the world, but most of them stick to warm places. If you have some trees in your garden you may be lucky—or unlucky—enough to see some. Long horned beetles can kill a tree. Their wormlike grubs burrow under the bark or deep into the wood. They can weaken large branches so much that they crash to the ground. The adult beetles behave a little better, eating the pollen in flowers and drinking the nectar. The male beetles spend a lot of time fighting over mates. Once a male has found a mate, he rides on her back for several hours to stop a rival from taking his place.

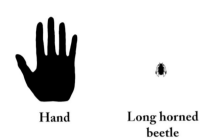

Hand

Long horned beetle

SIZE COMPARISON

▶ SOME OF THE LONG HORNED BEETLES that come out during the day are pretending to be wasps. They have the same banded pattern of yellow and black stripes, which is enough to scare off most predators.

Twig Girdlers

Some long-horned beetles are known as twig girdlers because of the way they provide food for their young. After the mother beetle has laid her eggs on a large twig, she nibbles away a ring of bark. That kills the twig, making it fall to the ground, ready for the grubs to eat.

Did you know?

• The titan beetle from the Amazon is the longest beetle in the world. It grows to 8in (20cm) long.

• The Asian long horned beetle is known as the starry sky beetle because it is black all over with small white spots.

• The eyes of the red milkweed beetle are split in two. The antennae grow out of the middle.

Millipede
Diplopoda

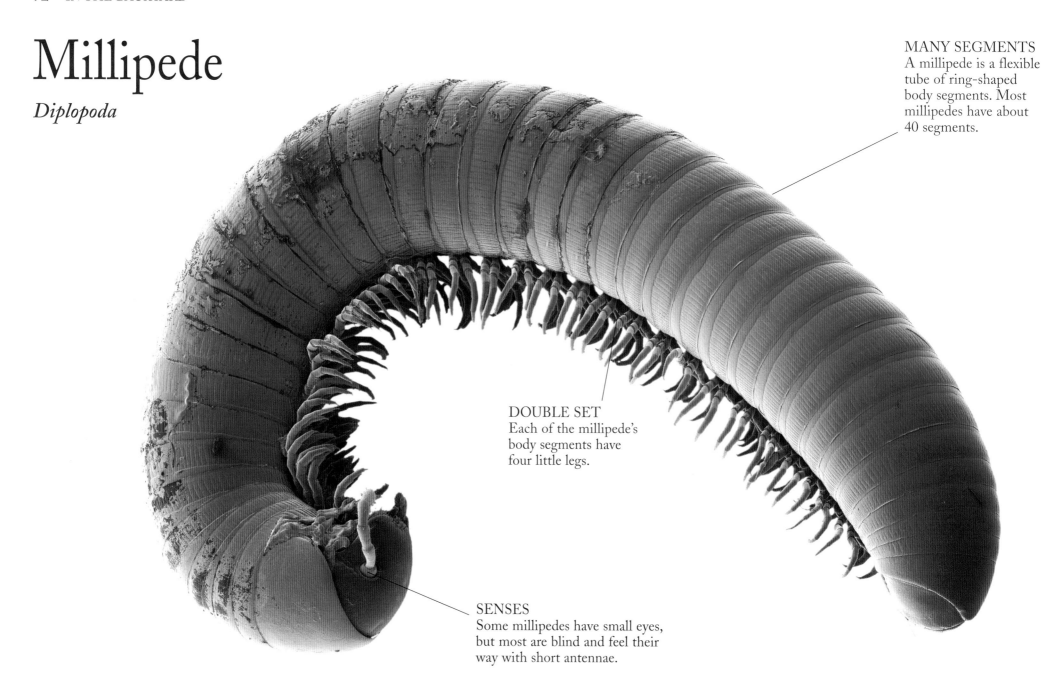

MANY SEGMENTS
A millipede is a flexible tube of ring-shaped body segments. Most millipedes have about 40 segments.

DOUBLE SET
Each of the millipede's body segments have four little legs.

SENSES
Some millipedes have small eyes, but most are blind and feel their way with short antennae.

The word millipede means "a thousand feet" and it is easy to see why they earned their name. Dozens of tiny legs look like a frilly drape surrounding the insect. When the legs move, this drape ripples, and the millipede seems to glide forward. However, most millipedes have nowhere near 1,000 legs. Most have about 80, although one large species has been counted with 800 legs! All millipedes are harmless. Most live underground or in piles of dead leaves, eating up rotting material. A few millipedes may be responsible for killing some garden plants, as they crop away at the tiny hairs that cover roots.

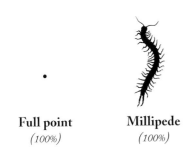

Full point
(100%)

Millipede
(100%)

SIZE COMPARISON

▶ GIANT AFRICAN MILLIPEDES are kept as pets all over the world. They grow to nearly 16in (40cm) long and can live for 10 years.

Shedding Skin

A young millipede has far fewer legs than its parents. As it grows, it must shed its old skin because it gets too small for it. Each time it changes its skin, the millipede adds another body segment—with four more legs. Large millipedes must shed their skin dozens of times to allow for all those legs.

Did you know?

• Some millipedes glow in the dark when a UV light is shone on them. Nobody really knows why—especially because most millipedes are blind!

• Army ants from South America keep millipedes as cleaners in the colony. In return, the fierce soldier ants protect the millipedes from attack.

Paper Wasp

Polistes sp

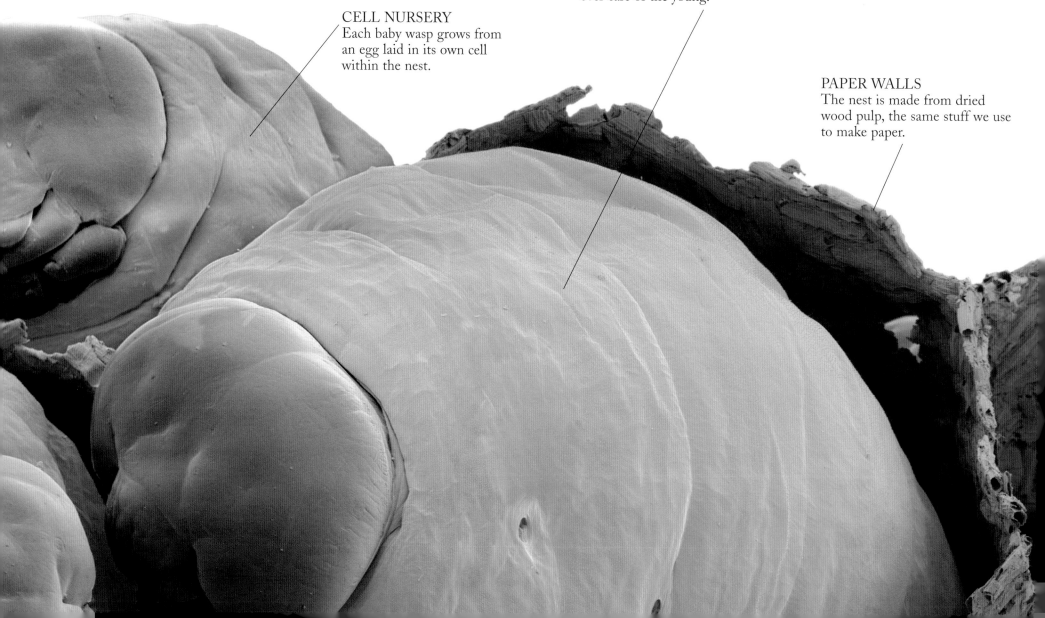

FEEDING TIME
Paper wasp larvae cannot feed themselves.
Their mother—the queen—will give them
half-digested insects and rotted meat. Once
they become adults, these daughters will take
over care of the young.

CELL NURSERY
Each baby wasp grows from
an egg laid in its own cell
within the nest.

PAPER WALLS
The nest is made from dried
wood pulp, the same stuff we use
to make paper.

Paper wasps are meat-eaters and kill other insects with their stings. They also slice off chunks of meat from dead animals. They are expert construction workers, too. They nibble off fibers of wood from trees and mix it with their spit to make a pulp cement. The pulp is sculpted into a honeycomb of hollow cells and left to dry, becoming a substance not unlike the paper used for this book. The hollow nest is light enough to hang from a single stalk, but also strong enough to keep out all but the bravest of attackers. Paper wasps will turn their stingers on anything that gets too close—including you!

Full point **Paper wasp**
(100 %) *(100%)*

SIZE COMPARISON

▶ MOST PAPER WASPS have the same black and yellow warning stripes as common wasps and hornets, but they have longer bodies with very narrow waists. In general, it is possible to call all these little stingers "paper wasps" because they build similar nests.

Nest Defense

A wasp nest is hung from a tree branch or perhaps a roof from a strong stalk. The wasps strengthen the stalk as the nest gets larger and heavier. They also coat it in a chemical that repels ants. Without this defense, ants would raid the nest and steal the eggs and tasty wasp larvae.

Did you know?

• Wasp nests can last for 25 years, long after the queen that founded it has died.

• Workers cool the nest in summer by crowding at the entrance and fanning air into it with their little wings.

• Once a queen is too old to rule the nest, one of her daughters kills her and starts to lay her own eggs.

Parasitic Wasp

Aphidius

FLEXIBLE BEHIND
The abdomen is very bendy so the wasp can jab an egg into an aphid from any angle.

SMELLING THE WAY
The wasp's antennae pick up chemicals released by a plant as a distress signal that it is under attack by aphids.

EGG TUBE
The ovipositor (egg-laying tube) is long and sharp to spear through an aphid's skin.

A parasite is an animal that lives on or inside another animal—known as its "host." Most wasps live like this. We usually think of wasps as stinging brutes that just won't buzz off. In fact, a wasp's stinger—and those of bees and ants—has evolved from the tube used to lay eggs. Parasitic wasps do not sting at all. They do something much worse. The lay an egg inside an animal—normally a spider or insect. The egg hatches into hungry wasp larvae, which eats its host from the inside. Once the host has been reduced to an empty husk, the baby wasp turns into an adult, climbs out, and flies off to find new hosts.

Full point
(Magnified 4 times)

Parasitic wasp
(Magnified 4 times)

SIZE COMPARISON

▶ ICHNEUMON WASPS are large parasitic wasps with a fierce-looking ovipositor. They are harmless to people, but lethal to a woodworm. The wasp's ovipositor is long and sharp enough to go through wood up to 1in (2.5cm) deep.

Searching for Grubs

The wasp searches for a grub hidden in the wood by patting the branch with its antenna. No one is sure, but it could be searching for the sounds made by a munching grub. She then drills her ovipositor into the wood with quick jabs until it reaches the grub's tunnel. The hatch wasp larva will not feed immediately. It waits until the grub is nice and juicy before eating it alive.

Did you know?

• One species of parasitic wasp is a parasite of a parasite: It eats the larvae of another wasp that is itself trying to devour a caterpillar. This is called hyperparasitism.

• Tarantula hawks are large parasitic wasps. They lay eggs inside tarantulas and then bury the host alive for the baby wasps to eat.

Scale Insect

Coccoidea

NO LEGS
This adult female scale insect lost her legs as she has grew. She does not need to walk again. All the food she will ever need is on the other side of the bark on which she sits.

WAXED BACK
The domed back is the platform for a waxy scale that is secreted from the skin.

NOT FOR LONG
This female is not quite fully grown. She will shed her skin one more time and lose her antennae.

A group of scales doesn't look like an insect at first. It looks more like odd mushrooms. But take a closer look. There are insects crawling on the scales. These are crawlers, the nymphs of the scales. Scale insects suck sap, and crawlers need a patch of bare bark to make their own. The female scale stays in one place for its adult life, protected by a waxy scale that can get so large it covers her in a hard dome. Only the male grows wings, and he flies away to mate with as many females as he can find. Within days, though, he will die. Some scale insects are hermaphrodites—both male and female at the same time.

Full point
(*Magnified 10 times*)

Scale insect
(*Magnified 10 times*)

SIZE COMPARISON

▶ THIS GANG OF SCALE INSECTS **is draining the sap that is stored inside a fleshy cactus plant. The cactus has turned white where the water and flesh has been drained away.**

Cochineal Insects

When Spanish exploters arrived in Central America in the sixteenth century, they were amazed by the bright red clothes the local Maya people wore. At that time, no one in Europe knew how to make such a deep red dye. At first, the Spanish thought the dye was made from moldy old cactus. In fact, it came from scale insects living on the plants. The scales are now known as cochineal bugs, and some red food dyes are still made from their crushed bodies.

Did you know?

• Early music records were made of shellac, a natural plastic produced by an Asian scale insect.

• Experts believe that the manna that saved Moses and the Israelites from starvation as they traveled through the desert was sweet wax produced by the tamarisk manna scale insect.

Slug
Gastropoda

BIG FOOT
Slugs walk on one foot, which carries them forward using a rippling motion. The foot is coated with watery mucus. This helps the slug slide and protects its soft body against rough ground.

HIDDEN SHELL
Most slugs do have a piece of shell, but it is very small and hidden under the animal's thick back section, or mantle.

TENTACLE
Slugs have four tentacles that can be pulled inside the body for safety—as they have been here. We can still see the stubs. The back pair are sensitive to light, while the ones farther forward pick up smell.

A slug is a snail without a home. Unlike its cousin, a slug has no shell to hide in. As well as being a refuge from attack, a shell stops the snail from drying out on hot days. Slugs must survive in other ways. They smear mucus all over themselves as a waterproof coat, and this also offers some protection from predators, as it makes them difficult to pick up. Slugs usually stay in a damp den on sunny days. The best time to see slugs is after heavy rain. They love to explore when it is nice and wet. Gardeners and farmers hate slugs because they eat leaves faster than a plant can grow, thus killing it.

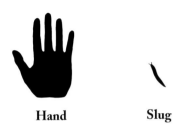

Hand   **Slug**

SIZE COMPARISON

▶ MOST SLUGS ARE plant-eaters. They can get through twice their bodyweight of leaves in one day. They scrape up food using a tongue covered in teeth.

Slug Slime

Slug slime is clever stuff. The trail of slime left behind is a calling card to any other slugs nearby. The smell of the slime tells them if the passing slug was a suitable mate. But some slugs are killers and use the slime to track their next meal. Thick mucus on the slug's back contains a natural anesthetic. Poke a slug, and the tip of your finger will go numb for several minutes. Native Americans wiped slug slime on sore teeth to make the ache go away.

Did you know?

• Slugs and snails are types of mollusks, which makes them relatives of the oyster and octopus.

• In Italy, people may swallow a slug to cure an upset stomach. It's a "cure" that often doesn't work.

• Slugs are male and female at the same time. Sometimes a pair's penises can get tangled up during mating and they have to bite them off to get free!

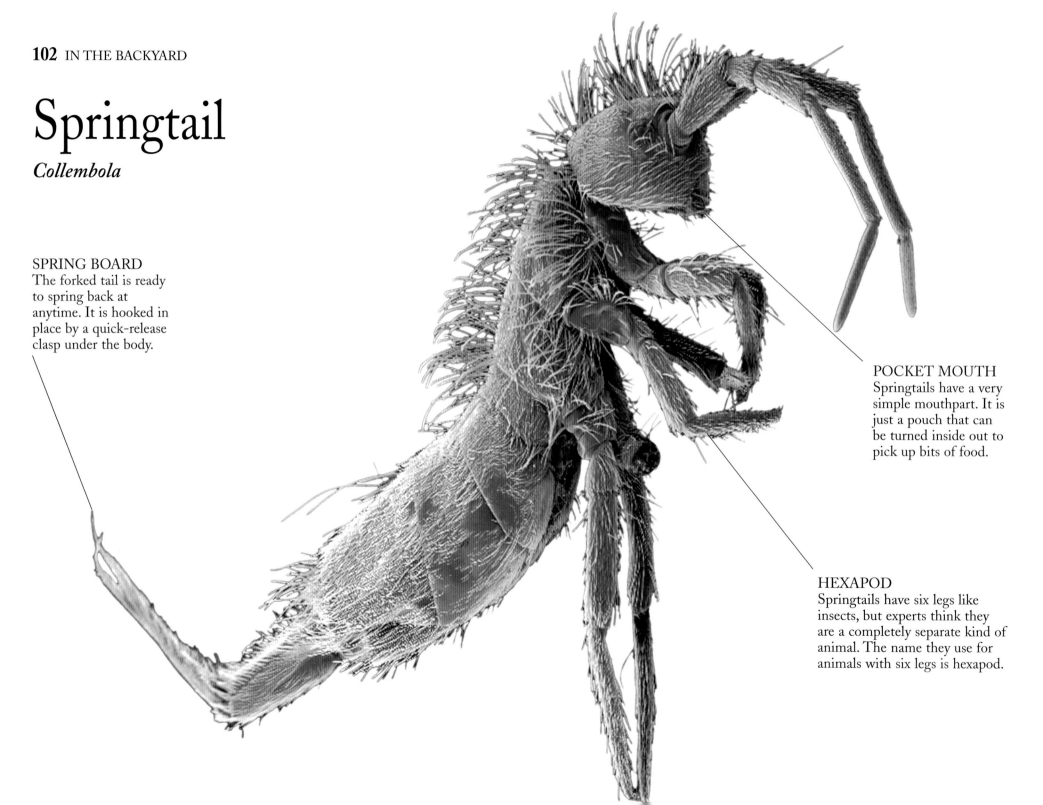

Springtail

Collembola

SPRING BOARD
The forked tail is ready to spring back at anytime. It is hooked in place by a quick-release clasp under the body.

POCKET MOUTH
Springtails have a very simple mouthpart. It is just a pouch that can be turned inside out to pick up bits of food.

HEXAPOD
Springtails have six legs like insects, but experts think they are a completely separate kind of animal. The name they use for animals with six legs is hexapod.

Now you see it, now you don't. Springtails are so small—just a few millimeters long—you will be lucky to spot one. And as soon as you do, it will probably disappear! They perform this trick with a flick of the tail. The tail is folded under the body most of the time, but when danger is near, it flips backward. That throws it high into the air—beyond the reach of an attacker. Springtails have lived on Earth for almost 400 million years, and have changed little. Their way of life works as well today as it did then. They eat just about anything and live just about everywhere on land—including Antarctica!

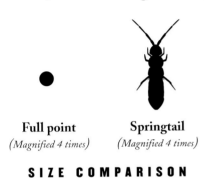

Full point
(Magnified 4 times)

Springtail
(Magnified 4 times)

SIZE COMPARISON

▶ AFTER SNOW IS a good time to spot springtails. At this time of year, they are known as snow fleas. They are one of the few minibeasts around in those conditions, and their dark bodies are easy to see against the white ground.

Millions of Springtails

The total number of springtails on Earth is enough to boggle your mind. Experts think that every 4 cups (1 liter) of soil has 1,000 springtails living in it. They are just so tiny that we rarely notice they are there. And the right kind of soil covers three-quarters of Earth's land. You do the math! The only other animals that live in such huge numbers are mites and worms.

Did you know?

• Springtails are small enough to swarm around on the surface of water—and their tail escape system still works perfectly.

• Springtails do not need to drink. They have a tube on their bellies that sucks up water from the ground.

Stinkbug

Palomena prasina

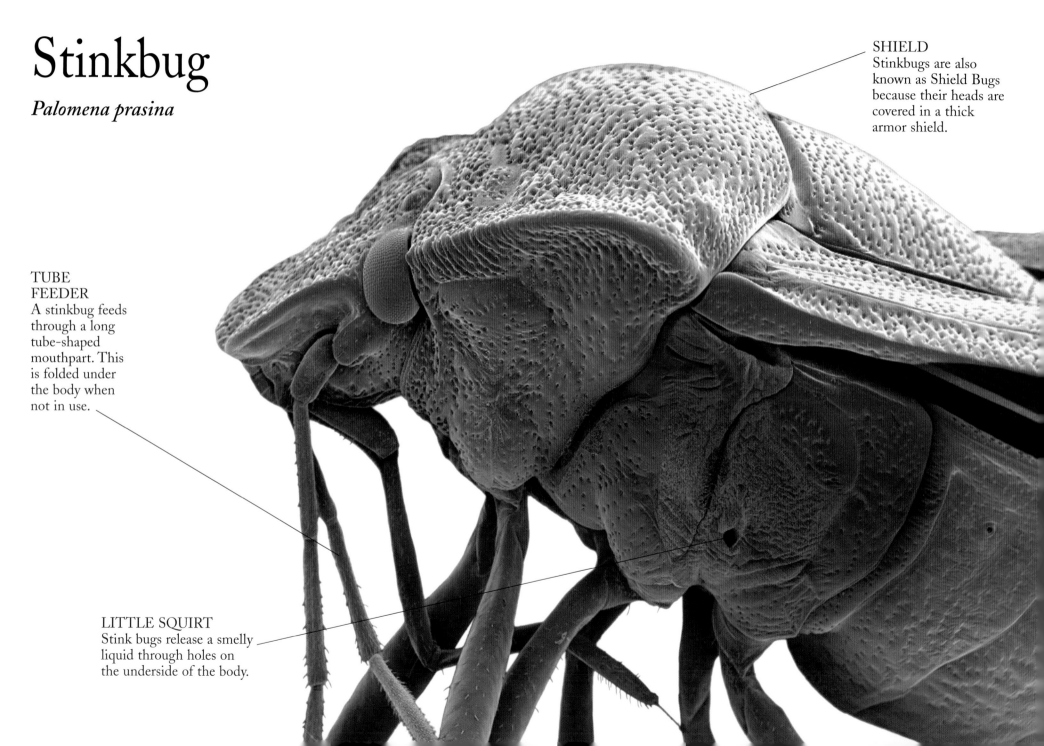

SHIELD
Stinkbugs are also known as Shield Bugs because their heads are covered in a thick armor shield.

TUBE FEEDER
A stinkbug feeds through a long tube-shaped mouthpart. This is folded under the body when not in use.

LITTLE SQUIRT
Stink bugs release a smelly liquid through holes on the underside of the body.

S tinkbugs are sap-suckers with boat-shaped bodies. You can tell them apart from a beetle because their wings poke out the end of a leathery covering. Stinkbugs attack crop plants, and if you grow tomatoes or lettuces, you are likely to have stinkbug visitors. Some stinkbugs are strong enough to pierce nutshells and drink the oils inside. Stinkbugs also cause a problem when you handle them. They are named after the way they squirt attackers with a smelly liquid from a gland between their first and second pair of legs. Some can squirt it quite a distance and with such force that it creates a popping sound.

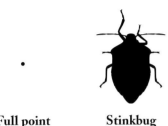

Full point
(100%)

Stinkbug
(100%)

SIZE COMPARISON

▶ NOT ALL STINKBUGS suck plant juice. The soldier bug sucks the juice out of other insects. Experts have enlisted this bug to fight a war against pests that damage crops. This bug is doing battle with a caterpillar on a tomato plant.

Digesting Food

Stinkbug nymphs hatch from their eggs as miniature versions of the parents, only without wings. The baby bugs feed on plant juices like their parents, but the first meal they have is sucking up a sticky liquid left on their soft egg shells by their mother. This liquid is full of bacteria, which will help them digest their food better.

Did you know?

• Indonesians eat roasted stinkbugs.

• The Sunn Pest is a stinkbug that causes serious problems for wheat farmers in the Middle East. Even if just a few percent of the wheat plants are affected by the bug, the whole crop is thrown away. Its flour will make the bread taste bad.

• Stinkbugs have antifreeze in their blood so they can survive winter frosts.

Thrips

Thysanoptera

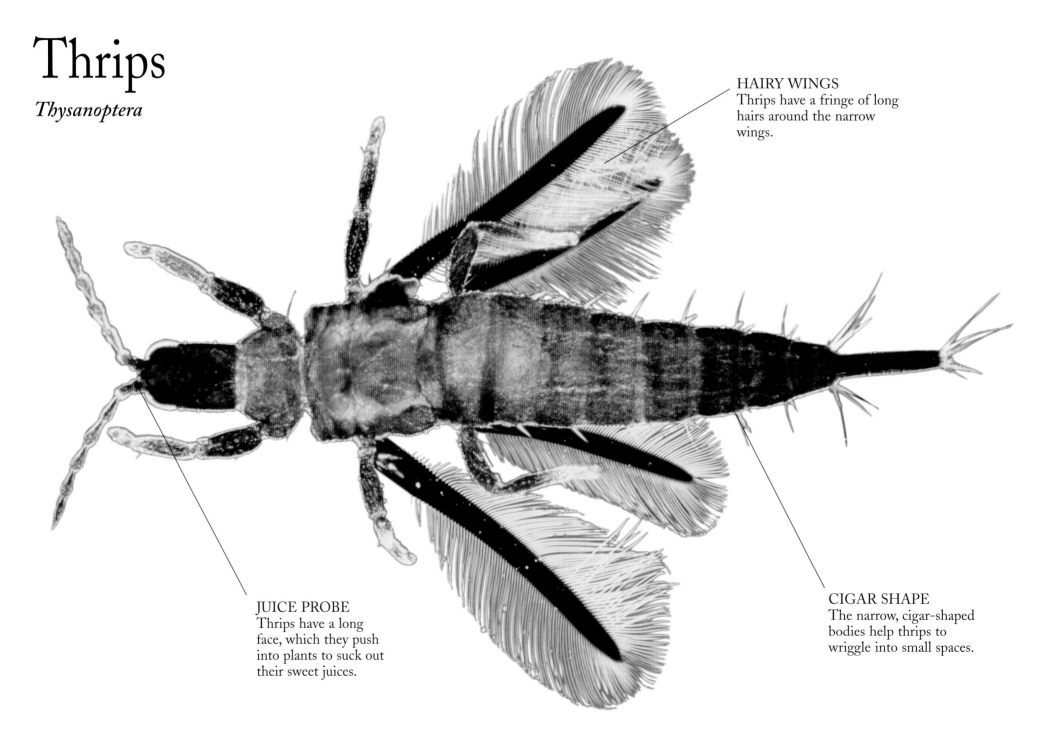

HAIRY WINGS
Thrips have a fringe of long hairs around the narrow wings.

JUICE PROBE
Thrips have a long face, which they push into plants to suck out their sweet juices.

CIGAR SHAPE
The narrow, cigar-shaped bodies help thrips to wriggle into small spaces.

hrips are tiny, plant-sucking flies. Don't be confused by the "s": A single one of these insects is still called a "thrips." These insects are not able to fly very fast themselves but they ride the wind for hundreds of miles. When the wind falls—as it does just before a heavy thunderstorm—thrips fall from the sky and crowd over flowers and fruits. As a result, many people know these little creatures as thunderbugs and storm flies. You rarely see a single thrips without seeing many more. They are a problem pest, creating ugly spots on fruits and vegetables and spoiling their appearance.

Full point
(Magnified 7 times)

Thrips
(Magnified 7 times)

SIZE COMPARISON

▶ BABY THRIPS, OR NYMPHS, look and live a lot like their parents. They do not have wings yet, but they feed by sucking juice from plants. Thrips multiply quickly. A female laying eggs in spring will become a great-great-grandmother by the autumn.

Baby Thrips

Thrips can reproduce by a male and female mating, or the female can just lay eggs without the help of a male. Normally, eggs laid by a non-mated female grow into identical copies of the mother—more females, in other words. However, thrips do it differently. Eggs produced by a female alone develop into a crowd of males. Only eggs created through mating will grow into female thrips.

Did you know?

• Thrips visiting some palm trees cause the plant to release a plume of pollen into the wind. The pollen is released only once the insects arrive.

• Thrips can smell when a hunting bug has killed a victim nearby. The thrips then dash for shelter inside the silk nests of mites.

Velvet Mite

Trombidiidae

STALK EYE
The mites are guided by two eyes held above the velvet hairs on stalks.

FINE HAIRS
Velvet mites get their shaggy look from hundreds of short bristles.

FANGS
The mites bite prey with two fangs that work like scissors.

The velvet mite is a mite with a difference—you can see it easily. Compared to most other mites, they are huge, growing to ¼in (5mm) across. And they are also bright red. The vibrant color is provided by carotenes—the same stuff that give carrots their orange color. The red is thought to be a warning to predators: "Don't eat this. It will make you sick." The system must work because large numbers of red velvet mites are found in most backyards, especially in the top layer of soil. They eat anything smaller than them, such as tiny insects and springtails. They also steal the eggs they find laid underground.

Full point
(Magnified 5 times)

Velvet mite
(Magnified 5 times)

SIZE COMPARISON

▶ A VELVET MITE LOOKS so velvety because each of its hairlike setae are highly branched so they create a thick coat over the body. Light is reflected from different parts of each bristle, giving the mite a glossy look.

The Young take it Easy

While adult velvet mites have to work hard to find food, the young take life a bit more easy. They suck the blood of grasshoppers, harvestmen, or just about anything else they can find. The baby mites have just six legs at this stage, and are a lot less furry. Once they have found a suitable supply of blood, the baby mites cling onto their host for several weeks. Only after a long drink of blood do the mites drop off and change into hunting adults.

Did you know?

• Red velvet mites are known as rain mites in India. They appear in huge numbers after the monsoon rains.

• A few types of young mite can bite humans and can cause a rash. People normally dismiss the bumps on their skin as a "heat rash."

Woodlouse

Armadillidium sp

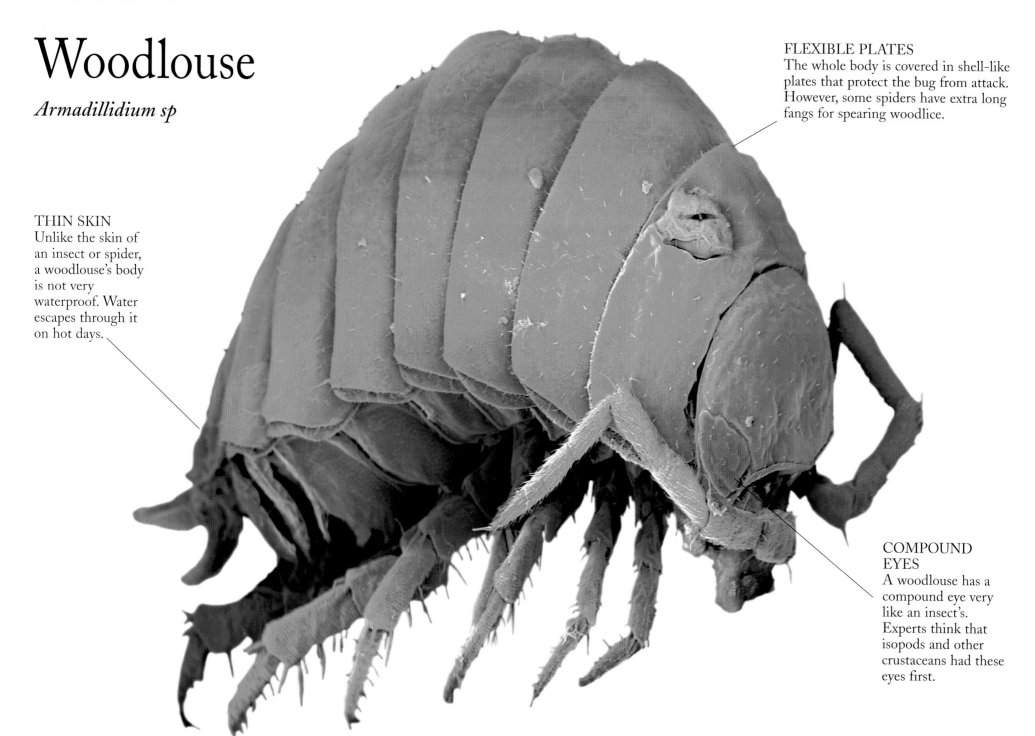

FLEXIBLE PLATES
The whole body is covered in shell-like plates that protect the bug from attack. However, some spiders have extra long fangs for spearing woodlice.

THIN SKIN
Unlike the skin of an insect or spider, a woodlouse's body is not very waterproof. Water escapes through it on hot days.

COMPOUND EYES
A woodlouse has a compound eye very like an insect's. Experts think that isopods and other crustaceans had these eyes first.

Woodlice belong to a group of animals called the isopods. Far from being cousins of insects or spiders, woodlice are actually more closely related to shrimp and barnacles. Most isopods live in the ocean, but a small group does well on land. With 14 clawed legs, they can crawl and climb just about anywhere. But they never stray too far from damp places. They prefer to come out at night and stay away from strong sunlight. Their sea-living cousins crawl across the seabed, eating the dead bodies that sink to the bottom. Woodlice live in much the same way, chewing up rotting leaves and dead animals.

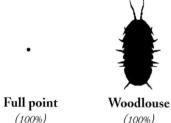

Full point (100%)   **Woodlouse** (100%)

SIZE COMPARISON

▶ THE WOODLOUSE IS ALSO known as a slater, pill bug, and roly poly. These last two names come from the way a few of them can roll up into an armored ball when attacked. Similar-looking sow bugs protect themselves with a squirt of nasty chemical that smells like rancid butter.

Sea Creatures

Although they live on land, woodlice are still sea creatures. They breath with gills held inside a damp chamber under the body. The bugs are constantly searching for water to keep the gills moist— otherwise they will suffocate in the air! Two spare feelers at the back of the bug suck up water from the ground. Sometimes woodlice explore indoors—they even climb stairs! But these adventurers are doomed. It is too dry for them, and they will soon curl up and die.

Did you know?

• Woodlice have a giant relative that is 14in (35cm) long—15 times the size of the ones in your backyard. As you might expect, it is a pretty tough customer. It needs to be—it lives more than 1 mile (2km) underwater!

• If you see a woodlouse that is bright blue, not gray, that means it is infected with a virus.

On the Body

I T MAY MAKE YOUR FLESH CREEP, your skin itch, and your hair stand on end, but there are dozens of micromonsters that are just hanging out to set up home on your body. Some want to suck your blood, others will nibble on your skin, but some want to burrow right into you and live on your internal organs! Never fear, though, because many of these disgusting critters are largely harmless and pretty rare. The worst thing that will probably happen is you will get a nasty nip from time to time an itchy rash. However, you may not realize it but your body is home to worms and mini mites that do so little harm you probably don't even know they are there. Many of these body pests were a much bigger problem in the past, when people did not have clean water and proper sewage systems. In general, we often think that only dirty people pick up these dirty bugs. That is only half true. Some of the micromonsters prefer you to be clean.

Biting Midge

Ceratopogonidae

TINY NIPPER
Biting midges are the smallest types of fly. They grow to just ¹⁄₂₅in (1mm) long and are small enough to wriggle through all but the finest nets.

LOW LIGHT
The large eyes are on the side of the head. Midges attack people in dark clothes more often than they do people wearing bright colors.

Other names for a midge are punkie or "no-see-um": these biting flies are so small they are hard to spot. If you meet some, though, you will know about it. A female midge gives a painful bite—and it will itch afterward. The midge wants your blood as a rich meal before she grows her eggs. Midges live in damp, wild places, like highland bogs and isolated beaches. No surprise, then, that hikers enjoying such spaces are often attacked. Midges cannot bite through clothing, so protect yourself by covering as much of your skin as possible—including wearing a hood made from netting over your face.

Full point
(Magnified 2 times)

Biting midge
(Magnified 2 times)

SIZE COMPARISON

▶ FEMALE BITING MIDGES have sharp, pointed mouths for piercing the skin. Their bodies become swollen as they gorge themselves on blood.

Muffleheads

In America, people may prefer to see a mufflehead instead of a punkie. Muffleheads are a type of midge that does not bite. They are just as small but have a fluffy tuft on their heads—hence the name. The tuft is the mufflehead's sensitive antennae. Muffleheads form annoying swarms in summer, and their red maggots crowd into pools of water. The maggots are colored by a chemical very similar to the one in our blood, and so they are called bloodworms.

Did you know?

• Biting midges spread African horse sickness, a virus that is harmless to people but is deadly to horses, donkeys, and zebras.

• Some people think eating Marmite, a type of yeast extract you spread on toast, makes biting midges think you smell bad.

• There is a midge forecast in Scotland, so walkers know to avoid the hills on particular days.

Eyelash Mite

Demodex folliculorum

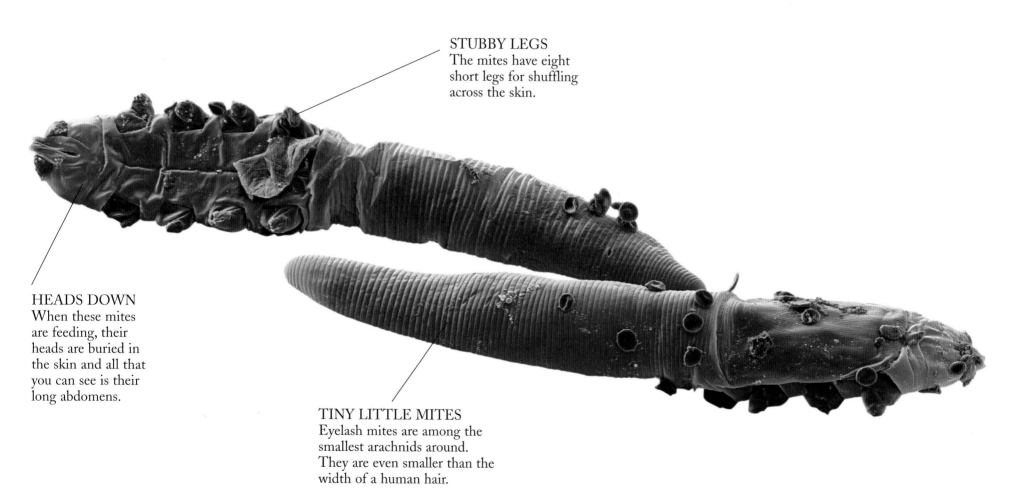

STUBBY LEGS
The mites have eight short legs for shuffling across the skin.

HEADS DOWN
When these mites are feeding, their heads are buried in the skin and all that you can see is their long abdomens.

TINY LITTLE MITES
Eyelash mites are among the smallest arachnids around. They are even smaller than the width of a human hair.

Do you have a pet? If you answer no, you may be wrong. You could easily be the proud owner of eyelash mites. About half of all people have mites living on the eyelashes and the fine hairs in the nose and ears. The mites are incredibly small: 10 could squeeze on to this period. The mites do not eat hair. Instead they graze on the skin cells and oils that line hair follicles. The eyelash mite has a close cousin—the Face Mite. It looks very similar but, instead of setting up home in hair follicles, they live in sebaceous glands. These are pockets in the skin which produce the oil that keeps skin smooth and supple.

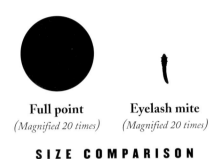

Full point	**Eyelash mite**
(Magnified 20 times)	*(Magnified 20 times)*

SIZE COMPARISON

▶ EYELASH MITES LOOK odd for arachnids (spiderlike creatures) because their abdomen has become long like a tail. They go for walks at night—they hate bright lights—looking for mates. Their top speed is 6¼in (16cm) per hour.

Mites and Allergies

Eyelash mites are completely harmless, although a few people suffer allergic reactions. However, a very similar mite causes mange in dogs and other pets. Only sick dogs are affected by mange, and humans never suffer from it. We are just not hairy enough!

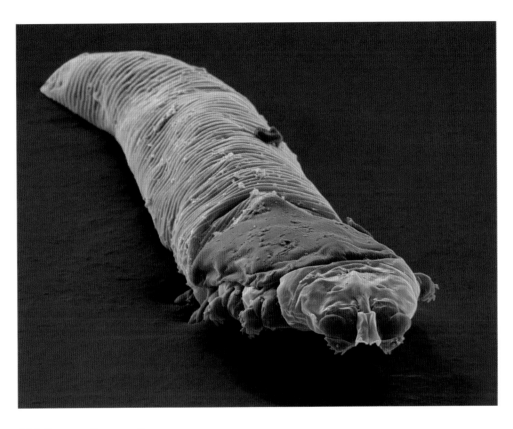

Did you know?

• The older you are, the more mites you have.

• Mites eat highly nutritious food. There is no waste left over, so they do not leave any droppings—they don't even have an anus!

• You can see your own mites by plucking an eyelash and looking at the end with a microscope.

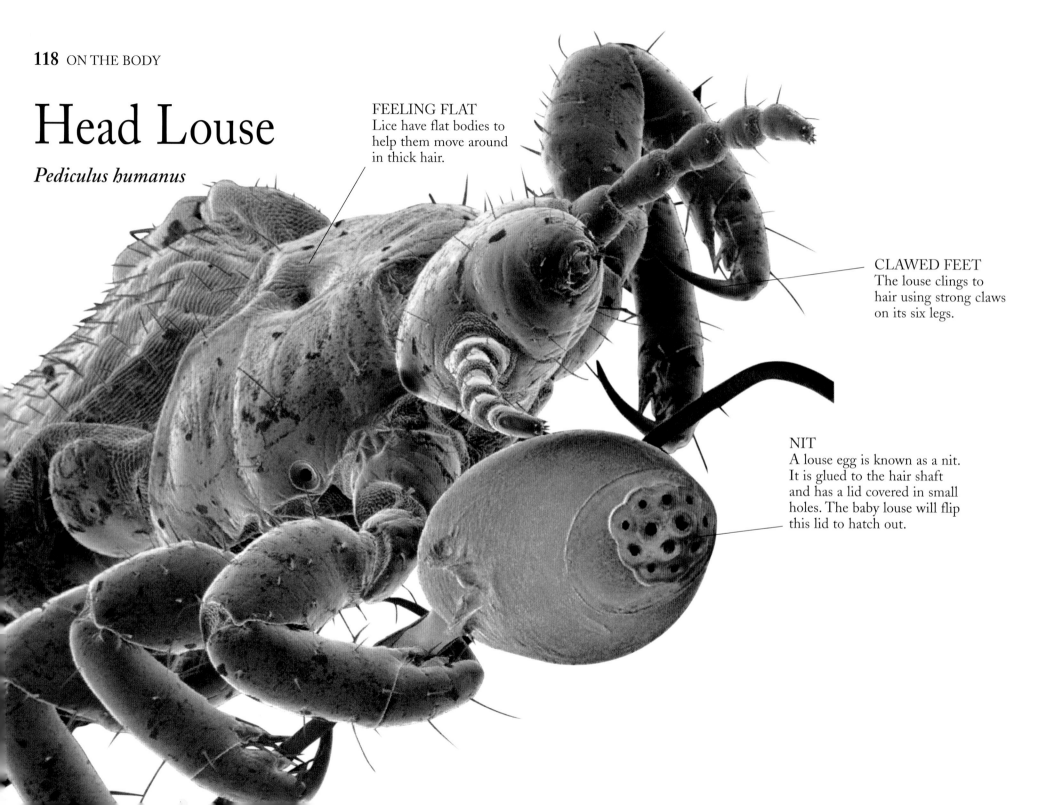

Head Louse

Pediculus humanus

FEELING FLAT
Lice have flat bodies to help them move around in thick hair.

CLAWED FEET
The louse clings to hair using strong claws on its six legs.

NIT
A louse egg is known as a nit. It is glued to the hair shaft and has a lid covered in small holes. The baby louse will flip this lid to hatch out.

Every year, hundreds of millions of people suffer from head lice. They may have an itchy head or feel tired—or they may feel nothing at all. Lice do not spread by jumping; they step from one head to another when people get close. They also cling to clothes, waiting for a chance to get to onto a head. Men can get lice in their beards, but head lice never venture below the neck. They prefer long hair, where they can wriggle unseen through the jungle of hair, sucking blood from the scalp and laying eggs. Washing hair doesn't get rid of lice—it just makes them clean. You need a treatment from the drugstore.

Full point
(Magnified 8 times)

Head louse
(Magnified 8 times)

SIZE COMPARISON

▶ MOST PEOPLE DO NOT REALIZE that they have head lice. However, people with long hair covering the back of the neck may get a rash of small pimples from the insects' bites.

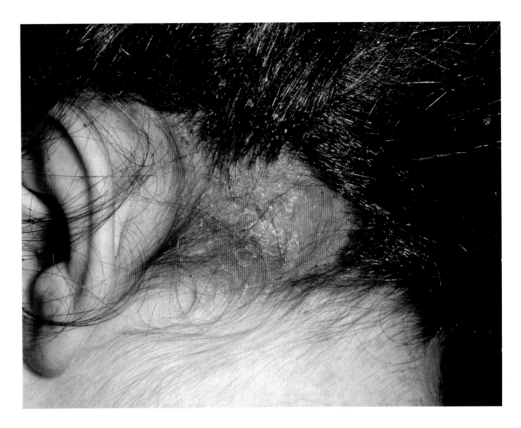

Times Two

No head lice treatment will kill 100 percent of lice and their eggs the first time. Chemical shampoos and sprays kill the active lice and no new eggs get laid, but the eggs already on the hairs are immune to attack. When these eggs have all hatched about 10 days later, it's time for a second treatment, which will hopefully kill them before they have the chance to lay fresh eggs.

Did you know?

• Feeling lousy today? You may have nits. Louse infestation brings you down a little, and that is probably where the word "lousy" comes from.

• Aztec peasants used to collect their head lice and give them to the emperor. It took so much work for people to collect them, it was seen as a worthy gift.

Hookworm

Ancylostoma duodenale

DOUBLE TEETH
Hookworms have two sets of teeth that gouge into the lining of the intestine.

BENT HEAD
Hookworms are so called because of the way the head bends at a slight angle to the rest of the body.

ROUNDWORM
Hookworms are a type of roundworm. Their bodies are not segmented into repeating sections like earthworms.

Hookworms make an amazing journey—through the human body. They are slender enough to burrow unseen into your skin—normally the feet. They ride the bloodstream around the body, until they pass through the heart and reach the lungs. The worms then dive into the phlegm lining the windpipe and are coughed up into the throat. Swallowed into the stomach, they set up home in the small intestines, sucking blood through the soft wall of the gut. The adult hookworms then lay eggs, which pass out with the solid waste. These eggs hatch, and the worms wait for a new victim.

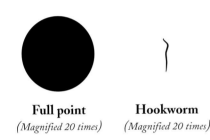

Full point
(Magnified 20 times)

Hookworm
(Magnified 20 times)

SIZE COMPARISON

▶ HOOKWORMS CAN GET into our bodies through dirty foods, but most of them burrow into our feet. They leave a red trail as they look for a large blood vessel to take them deep into the body.

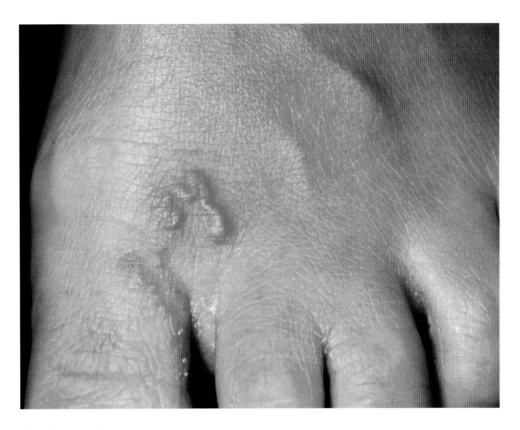

Reducing Allergies

Our body is good at fighting off attack—perhaps too good in some cases. Some doctors think that common allergies such as asthma and hayfever are caused by the body's defenses reacting as if under attack. People with a few hookworms are half as likely to suffer from allergies. The worms give the body something real to fight against.

Did you know?

• Bad infestations of hookworms are called miner's anemia or tunnel disease because the worms thrive in the warm sandy soils inside deep earthworks. Sufferers go a little green.

• Doctors in ancient Egypt thought hookworms made people go slightly mad.

• More than one in 10 people are home to hookworms.

Human Flea

Pulex irritans

WINGLESS
Great jumpers do not need wings, which would get in the way when the flea was moving across hairy bodies.

SUCKING MOUTH
The flea squirts saliva into the wound through its sharp mouthpart to keep the blood flowing. That is how it passes on diseases.

OFF THE KNEES
Fleas jump from a kneeling position so that they can maximize the force of their springy legs.

That's right, humans have their very own type of flea. However, human fleas are not fussy and will live on just about any other mammal. The fleas of other animals—especially cats and dogs—also bite us, but they tend to nip just our legs. Only human fleas attack the whole body. Barely $\frac{1}{25}$in (1mm) long, they look just like dark dots. The insects make enormous leaps—150 times their own body length—to reach the warm body of a host. The adults are bloodsuckers, but the baby fleas are hairy ground-living worms. They eat anything edible among the dust, but prefer the blood-rich droppings of older fleas.

Full point
(Magnified 7 times)

Human flea
(Magnified 7 times)

SIZE COMPARISON

▶ A HUNDRED YEARS AGO, flea circuses were a top attraction. Circus fleas are fitted with a wire harness. As this one tries to jump free, its powerful back legs will kick the tiny "soccerball," and it will appear as if the insect is taking a shot at the goal.

The Black Death

The rat flea is a close relative of the human flea—and about 650 years ago it helped to kill one-fifth of the human population on Earth! Rat fleas spread the Black Death, or bubonic plague. These fleas do not usually bite people, but when they become infected with plague bacteria they are driven mad with hunger and they will bite anything they can. There are a few plague cases even today, but modern medicine can treat them.

Did you know?

• When a flea jumps, it accelerates 50 times faster than a space rocket.

• Young fleas do not hatch from their cocoons until they sense the body heat or breath of a large animal nearby. They quickly hatch out and make a jump for it.

• Fleas have stretchy bodies. Otherwise, the force of a jump would rip them open.

Leech

Hirudo medicinalis

MOUTH
The mouth is inside a smaller sucker at the thinner end of the animal.

BODY BREATHER
Leeches do not breathe. All the oxygen they need passes straight into the body through the damp skin.

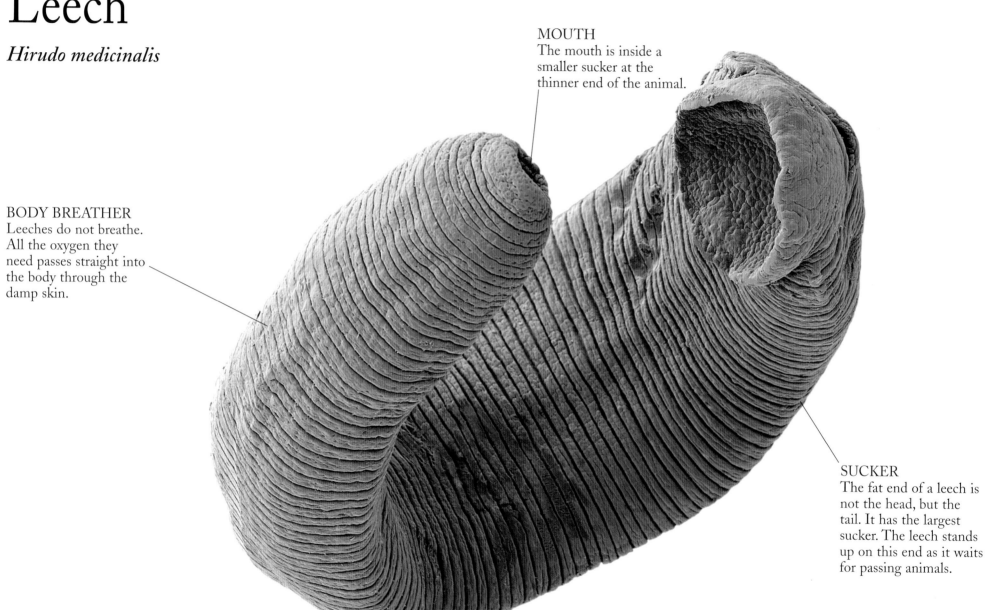

SUCKER
The fat end of a leech is not the head, but the tail. It has the largest sucker. The leech stands up on this end as it waits for passing animals.

Leeches are blood-sucking worms. Most live in the ocean, but they are also found in swamps and hot and damp areas of land, especially jungles. Biting land leeches will spend days waiting for their next meal beside a forest track. When an animal—or a person—strolls past, the leech grabs hold with its head sucker. It then shuffles on its suckered tips to a feeding place. Thanks to painkillers in the saliva, you won't feel the bite. The saliva also contains a chemical that stops your blood from clotting. Once the leech is swollen with blood, it falls to the ground—but the bite may keep bleeding for a while.

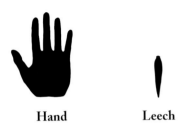

Hand   **Leech**

SIZE COMPARISON

▶ LEECHES ARE SUCH GOOD suckers that doctors attach them to wounds. The worms pull fresh blood through the damaged area, and this helps to speed up healing. Leeches are especially useful for fixing bad cuts on fingers and toes.

How to Remove a Leech

Leeches do not burrow into the body, they just suck on the skin, so they are quite easy to remove. However, if you give one a tug, you may force the blood back out of its the mouth. That could burst the head, leaving pieces of mouth stuck in the skin. What you need to do is convince the leech to stop feeding before you pull it off. Heat from a flame works but could also hurt you. Salt, spit, and fruit juice will also do the trick.

Did you know?

• Doctors once thought that illnesses were caused by having too much blood. They used leeches to suck out the extra blood.

• Scientists copy the chemicals in leech saliva to make drugs that stop blood clots from forming in sick people.

• Leeches feed only two or three times a year.

Liver Fluke

Fasciola hepatica

BLIND ALLEY
The fluke's mouth leads to a dead-end compartment. The animal does not produce droppings. Every bit of its food is used by the body.

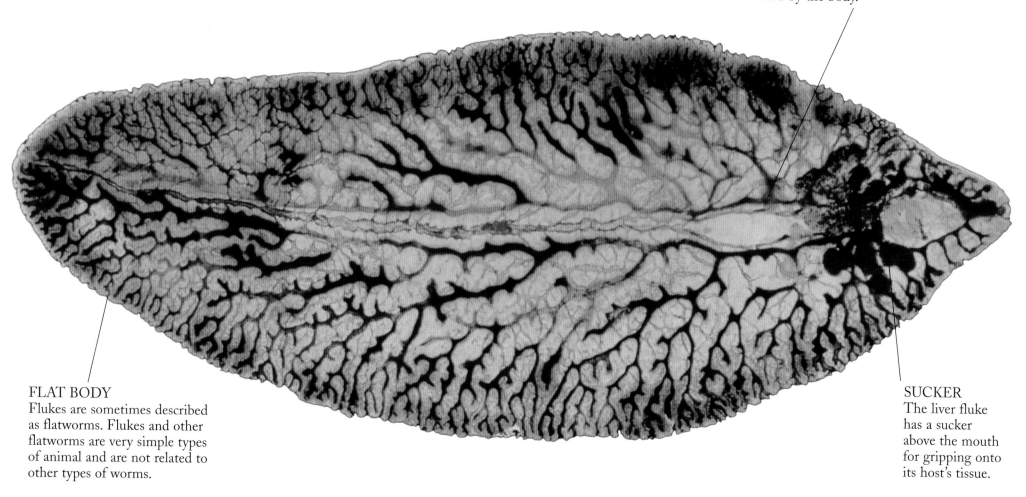

FLAT BODY
Flukes are sometimes described as flatworms. Flukes and other flatworms are very simple types of animal and are not related to other types of worms.

SUCKER
The liver fluke has a sucker above the mouth for gripping onto its host's tissue.

Eating salad is good for you—most of the time. Liver flukes are wormlike creatures that live inside the bodies of grass-eating farm animals, such as sheep and cows. They can also get into humans who eat some kinds of unwashed salad greens, including watercress. The fluke begins life inside a water snail. It then swims away and takes up position on a plant beside the water. Their leaves might end up on your plate. Once inside the body, the fluke burrows out of your gut and sets up home in the liver. It lives there for a few weeks before heading back to the digestive system to release eggs in your waste.

Full point
(100%)

Liver fluke
(100%)

SIZE COMPARISON

▶ ONE TYPE OF FLUKE seeks out humans on purpose and lives in our blood vessels. Schistosome flukes cause a sickness called bilharzia, or snail disease. Symptoms of bilharzia vary from tiredness to bladder cancer. The worms can be killed with drugs.

Mates for Life

Like liver flukes, schistosome flukes spend time inside snails before burrowing into people swimming in swampy rivers. Male schistosome flukes are much large than the females. When mates meet, the female lives inside a groove on the male's body.

Did you know?

• A sheep infected with a fluke could have half a million worm eggs in its dung. Most will never make to the next stage of their lives.

• The name "fluke" comes from the Old English word for flounder—a flat fish that looks similar to the worm.

• Giant liver flukes grow to 4in (10cm) long and 1¼ in (3cm) wide—the size of a small chocolate bar.

Sand Flea

Tunga penetrans

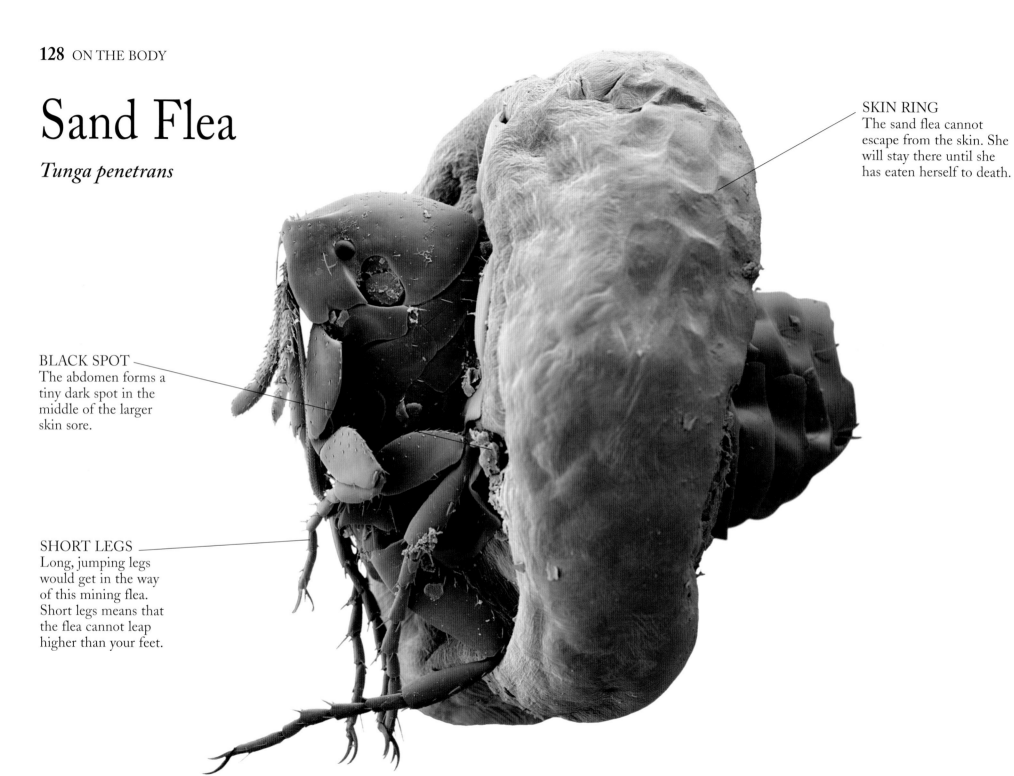

SKIN RING
The sand flea cannot escape from the skin. She will stay there until she has eaten herself to death.

BLACK SPOT
The abdomen forms a tiny dark spot in the middle of the larger skin sore.

SHORT LEGS
Long, jumping legs would get in the way of this mining flea. Short legs means that the flea cannot leap higher than your feet.

Compared to its bionic cousins, the sand flea is small and wimpy. It grows to less than ¹⁄₂₅in (1mm) long and can jump to only ¾in (2cm) off the ground. But do not be fooled, the sand flea—or jigger—is a nasty little thing. The female flea does not just sip your blood, she burrows into the skin to get a bellyfull. She gets in so deep that all that can be seen is the tip of her abdomen. She can breathe through this body part as the rest of her body swells up with blood under the skin, eventually forming a pale round sore. The flea will literally drink until she bursts, and will then release hundreds of eggs that fall to the ground.

Full point
(Magnified 20 times)

Sand flea
(Magnified 20 times)

SIZE COMPARISON

▶ SAND FLEAS LURK in sandy soil until a host comes past. They normally attack feet, so the best defense is to wear closed shoes, not sandals.

Two Types of Chiggers

Sand fleas live in South America. They are also called jiggers, chigoe fleas, and sometimes chiggers. They should not be confused with harvest mites, which are better known as chiggers in North America. These also attack people, but not for their blood; they just gnaw away at the skin cells.

Did you know?

• If people leave their sand flea bites to get infected, they could die from blood poisoning.

• People who have been attacked by a lot of sand fleas may end up with lumpy scars on their feet, and these can be painful.

• Doctors kill fleas in the skin by applying liquid nitrogen—it is very cold and freezes them instantly.

Scabies Mite

Sarcoptes sp

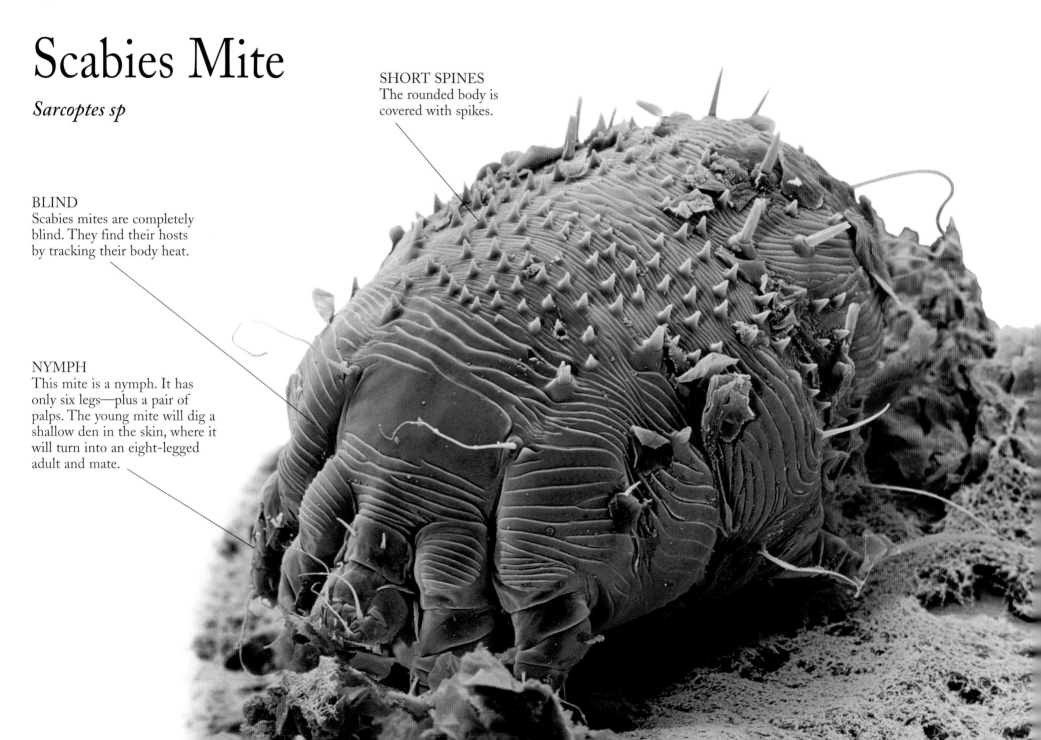

SHORT SPINES
The rounded body is
covered with spikes.

BLIND
Scabies mites are completely
blind. They find their hosts
by tracking their body heat.

NYMPH
This mite is a nymph. It has
only six legs—plus a pair of
palps. The young mite will dig a
shallow den in the skin, where it
will turn into an eight-legged
adult and mate.

Also known as the itch mite, this minute insect causes a skin condition called scabies. Scabies is the human version of dog mange. However, it is a lot less common. Most dogs have at least a few mites on them, but only about one in every thousand people has a scabies mite problem. The mites pass from one person to another when their skin touches for a long time. The most common way is through holding hands, and most scabies mites are found on the hand and wrist. The titchy mites burrow into the skin, causing an itchy rash. The mites—and their rash—will spread across the body.

Full point
(Magnified 20 times)

Scabies mite
(Magnified 20 times)

SIZE COMPARISON

▶ ONLY THE FEMALE MITES burrow deep into your skin. They use the long tunnels as nurseries for their eggs. The itching is caused by a reaction to the mites' saliva and droppings.

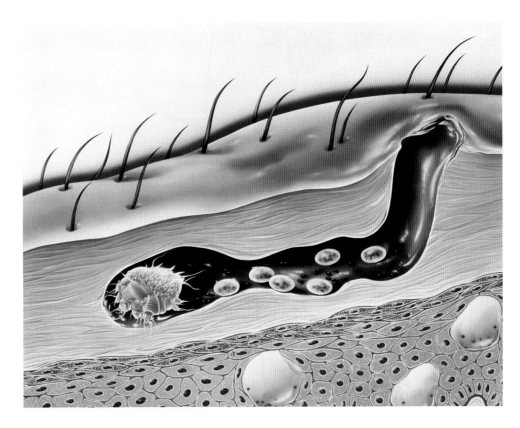

An Early Diagnosis

Scabies is thought to be one of the first diseases in history to have its cause correctly identified. As early as the third century B.C.E., Aristotle recorded that "lice" escaped from the pimples on the skin. The disease was named by the Romans—"scabies" comes from the Latin for "scratch." In the seventeenth century, an Italian doctor called Giovanni Cosimo Bonomo made the link between the mite and the rash.

Did you know?

• The first recording of scabies comes from *Leviticus*, a book in the Torah and Bible, which was written about 3,000 years ago.

• Female scabies mites are just 0.5mm long, which is twice as big as the males.

• Human itch mites also attack pigs.

Stable Fly

Stomoxys calcitrans

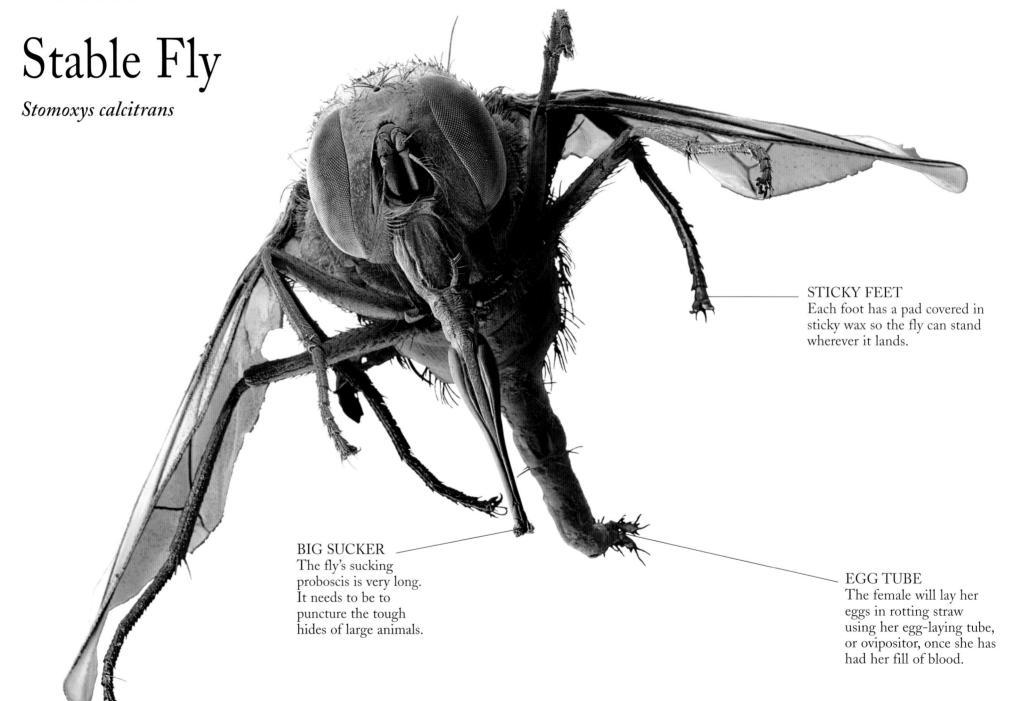

STICKY FEET
Each foot has a pad covered in sticky wax so the fly can stand wherever it lands.

BIG SUCKER
The fly's sucking proboscis is very long. It needs to be to puncture the tough hides of large animals.

EGG TUBE
The female will lay her eggs in rotting straw using her egg-laying tube, or ovipositor, once she has had her fill of blood.

The stable fly lives in outbuildings that shelter animals. It is a close relatives of the house fly, and it will give you a nasty bite. It sucks the blood of large mammals, which is why it is found around stables and barns. It is only the females that drink blood. They need the nutritious food to make a large clutch of eggs. The flies search for a suitable animal. They land on the back first and then move to the legs, neck, or belly to feed. If the fly is disturbed while feeding, she will fly off a short distance before returning to the open bite. Once you are bitten, it will take a while before the fly leaves you alone!

Full point
(100%)

Stable fly
(100%)

SIZE COMPARISON

▶ STABLE FLIES SHOULD NOT be confused with horseflies. Both feed on the blood of horses—and their stable hands—but horseflies are considerably large and meaner.

Outsize Eyes

A horsefly is twice the size of a stable fly. And they have big eyes to match, among the largest of any insect. The eyes almost cover the whole head. You can tell a male from a female horsefly because there is no gap at all between the two eyes.

Did you know?

• Stable flies sometimes come in to farmhouses in bad weather.

• The flies may spread anthrax and other farm diseases.

• You can tell a stable fly from a house fly by the stripes on its back.

Tapeworm

Taenia pisiformis

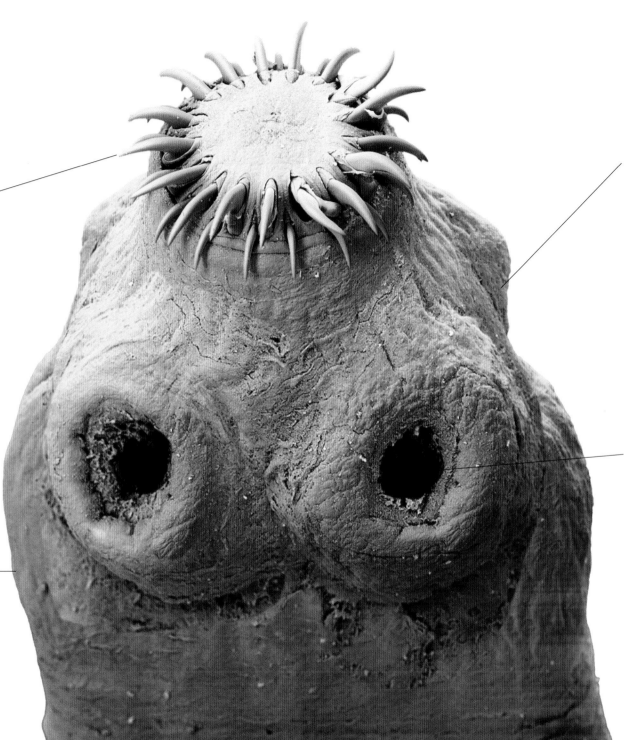

HOOKED HEAD
Tapeworms hold
onto the lining of
their victim's
instestines using a
frill of hooks called
a scolex.

NO MOUTH
The worm does not
have a mouth. It just
absorbs food through
its skin in the same
way that the lining of
the gut works.

HOLD ON
Two suckers hold on
to the wall of the gut.

IN DISGUISE
The worm covers its body
in the same chemicals that
cover the intestine. That
way, the body's defense
force will not see it as
an invader.

Do you like your steak rare? You may change your mind after reading this. Tapeworms are long, flat parasites that live coiled up in your intestines. They get there after you eat some meat containing tapeworm cysts. If the meat is only lightly cooked, some of those cysts will be alive as you eat. A cyst gradually grows into a worm that could be your secret companion for years. Most tapeworms do not cause problems unless they get so big that they block your intestines. People catch tapeworms by eating beef or pork. However, tapeworms are rare. In most countries, the meat is checked for cysts before it is sold.

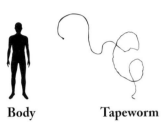

Body   **Tapeworm**

SIZE COMPARISON

▶ THE TAPEWORM is attached to the gut at the thin end (in the center of this ring). The other end of the worm is thicker and divided into segments. These steadily fall off and pass out of the body, ready for another animal to eat them.

Hungry for Lions

Tapeworms want to get into top predators—like lions. The beef tapeworm is happy to reach the guts of humans. However, pork tapeworms have other ambitions. To them, we are too similar to the pig they just came from. So they form cysts in our muscles—and then wait for a lion to eat us. Obviously, that does not happen very often, so the cysts just get bigger and can cause serious health problems if left untreated.

Did you know?

• Tapeworms can grow to many feet inside an intestine.

• Anti-tapeworm drugs paralyze the worm so that it cannot hold on anymore. It passes out of the gut with natural waste.

• The risks of catching a pork tapeworm is thought to be one of the reasons why so many cultures refuse to eat pigs.

Threadworm

Trichostrongylus vitrinus

PIN TAIL
The narrow, pointed end is the back of the worm.

SUPER SLENDER
As their name suggests, threadworms are very thin. They are almost see-through.

WRIGGLING
Threadworms wriggle wildly from side to side. That is all their simple muscles can do for them. They crawl through the gut at about 6in (15cm) per hour.

Don't bite your nails! They will get sore and look ugly—and may have threadworm eggs under them. Threadworms—also called pinworms—are roundworms. Just a few millimeters long, they are the most common parasite in the world. One in 10 people has them living inside their intestines. The worms are harmless, and just cause itching now and then. They enter the body as eggs through the mouth. The eggs hatch once they reach the small intestine. After a few weeks, the worms mate. The males then die, but the females head down to the colon—the large intestine—and produce the next generation.

Full point
(Magnified 5 times)

Threadworm
(Magnified 5 times)

SIZE COMPARISON

▶ THREADWORMS COME OUT at night. The tiny wrigglers come out of the bottom to lay their eggs. They then head back inside to the large intestine. People with threadworms often feel itchy around bedtime.

Infecting Ourselves

Anyone can catch threadworms. They spread most quickly between young children who are still learning how to stay clean. And children can then pass the eggs on to older people. Once you have threadworms, washing with soap will have no effect. Most of the infection comes from yourself as the tiny and super-sticky eggs are transferred from the bottom to the mouth. However, a couple of pills is enough to kill all the worms.

Did you know?

• Threadworm eggs must be laid on the outside of the body so the eggs can get the air they need to develop properly.

• Dead worms become opaque (they stop being see-through).

Under Water

MICROMONSTERS ARE NOT ONLY FOUND ON LAND. They are just as at home in rivers, streams, and even in the deep ocean. Out in the wide open water, micromonsters are not quite so tiny. They may start out too small to see, but they just get bigger and bigger. In the case of jellyfish they may grow to be bigger than a person. Other water beasts stay hidden for most of the time, but wherever they are life is disgusting, bizarre, and downright dangerous.

Ponds may seem calm places above the surface. But down below, baby dragonflies and diving beetles are terrorizing the wildlife. Pond snails are well protected by a tough shell, and caddisflies build their own armored mobile home. Out at sea, things get a bit wilder. Jellyfish are well named. They are little more than a bag of jelly—but they are still alive! And just like back on land, sea worms wriggle under the seabed. The difference is they are frilly and poisonous.

Life in water is very different to life on land, and taking a peek under the surface opens up a whole new world of monsters.

Brine Shrimp

Artemia salina

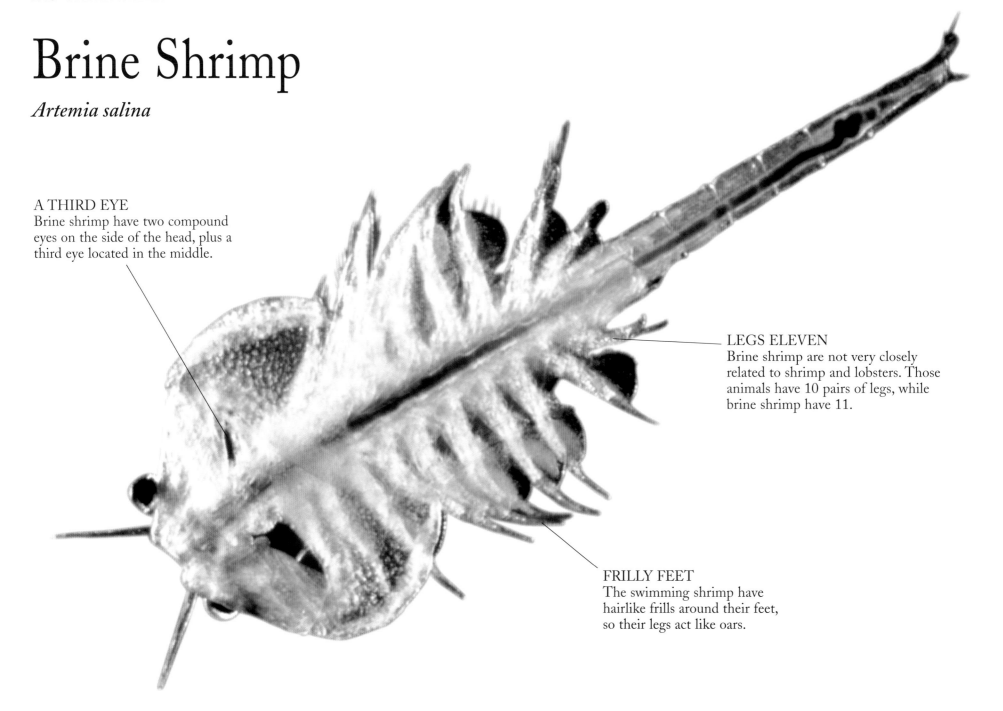

A THIRD EYE
Brine shrimp have two compound
eyes on the side of the head, plus a
third eye located in the middle.

LEGS ELEVEN
Brine shrimp are not very closely
related to shrimp and lobsters. Those
animals have 10 pairs of legs, while
brine shrimp have 11.

FRILLY FEET
The swimming shrimp have
hairlike frills around their feet,
so their legs act like oars.

Brine shrimp are tiny relatives of krill, shrimp, and crabs. But you won't find any in the sea. "Brine" is another word for "saltwater," and although seawater is brine, the brine in desert lakes is much stronger. As the desert heat makes the water evaporate, the salt stays behind, making these lakes the saltiest places on Earth.

Welcome to the home of brine shrimp. They eat bacteria and algae that grow in hot, salty places. If their lake dries up completely, their eggs turn into tough cysts that can survive without water, light, or air. They can even be frozen. The eggs will still hatch as soon as they get wet again.

Full point
(Magnified 3 times)

Brine shrimp
(Magnified 3 times)

SIZE COMPARISON

▶ BRINE SHRIMP LAY two types of egg. When the water is deep and not too salty, they lay eggs with thin shells that hatch immediately. If the amount of salt in the water is going up, that means the pool will soon dry out completely, so the female shrimp lay eggs with thick shells that can cope without water.

Sea Monkeys

You say "brine shrimp," I say "sea monkey." Brine shrimp eggs are often sold as "sea monkey" powder—just add water and see live animals appear from nowhere! A home sea-monkey pool needs specially clean water and certain salts, and then, if you are lucky, your flock of sea monkeys will grow to ½in (1cm) long and live for a year. But of course, now you know that sea monkeys do not come from the sea at all!

Did you know?

• Brine shrimp will die in tap water mixed with table salt from the kitchen. There is a tiny amount of iodine added to our table salt. This keeps us healthy but it kills the shrimp.

• Baby brine shrimp swim using their large antennae.

Bristleworm

Amphinomidae

POISONOUS BRISTLES
The bristleworm is a fireworm—a name that comes from poison in the bristles on the tips of its "feet." Touching the worm produces a burning sensation.

BODY SEGMENTS
Bristleworms are distant relatives of earthworms and leeches. Like them, the body is divided into several repeating sections.

ON THE SIDE
It might look like the worm has legs or feet, but these side sections are called parapodia, meaning "almost feet."

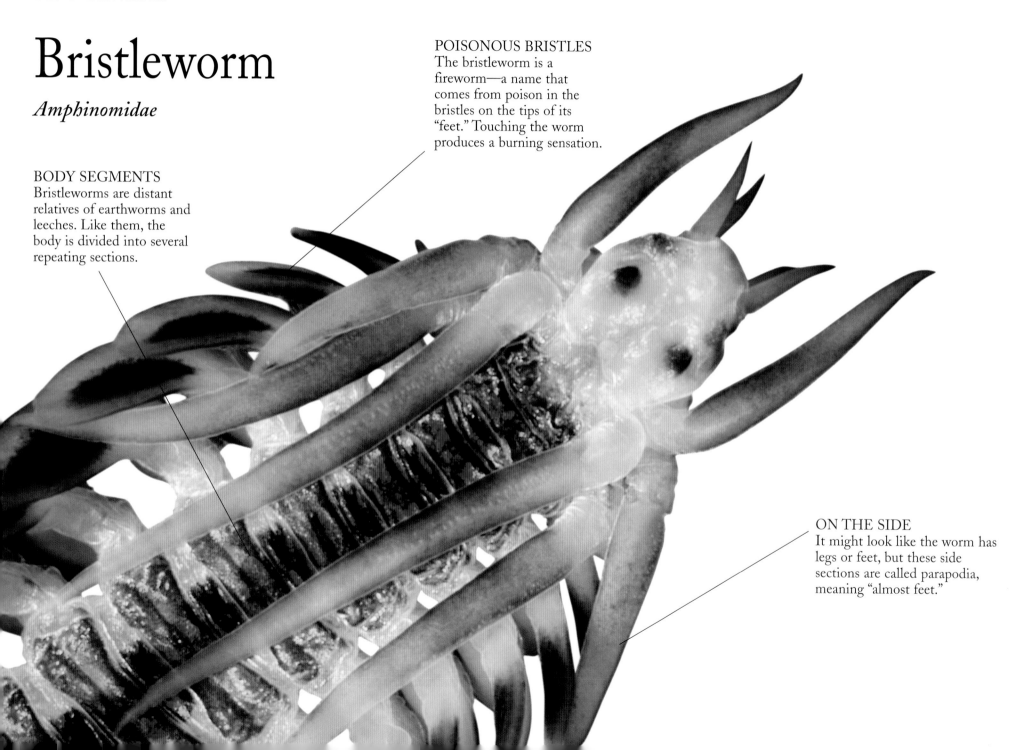

Undersea worms are hairier than the ones on land. They are known as bristleworms, and most are found deep down on the bottom of the ocean floor. In fact, a tiny worm was found living on the seabed of the Marianas Trench, the lowest point in the Earth's ocean. However, there are billions of bristleworms much closer to home. The next time you are on a wet sandy beach, look for worm-shaped coils of sand. This is not a worm itself, but a plaster-cast made from its sandy waste. The worm is burrowing under the sand. You could try to dig it out but it could be more than 20in (50cm) down.

Hand

Bristleworm

SIZE COMPARISON

▶ CHRISTMAS TREE WORMS live in coral reefs. One end of the worm is attached to a rock and a spiral of bristles along the body makes it look like a pine tree. The bristles sift food from the water.

Hot Water

Some of the largest bristleworms live in darkness at the very bottom of the sea. Tubeworms 10ft (3m) long are found around black smokers—super-hot springs on the seabed near undersea volcanoes. The hot water contains chemicals, but the tubeworm cannot make use of them. However, inside its body are bacteria that can. The worms use a plume of bristles to collect the chemicals for them. The bacteria then provide the worm with food.

Did you know?

• Some bristleworms change their bodies into swimming forms so they can get together to breed. However, the swimming worms do not have working stomachs, so they will soon die of starvation.

• Bristleworms drill into the bones of dead whales to feed.

• Tubeworms grow very slowly and can live for more than 100 years.

Brittle Star

Ophiocoma wendtii

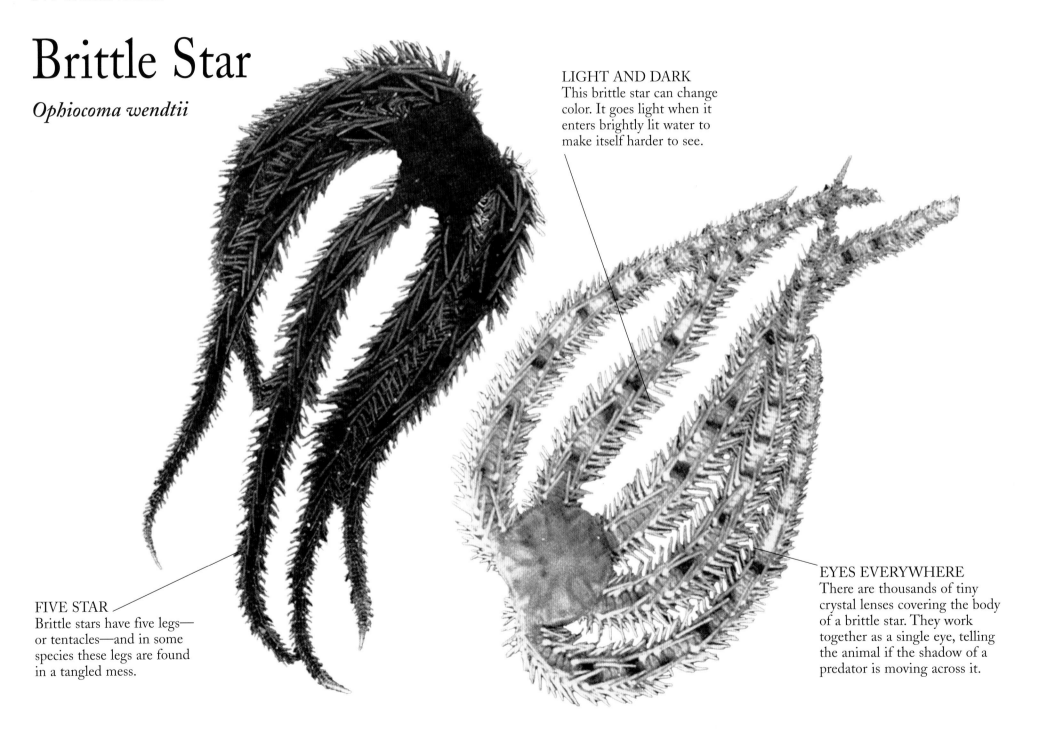

LIGHT AND DARK
This brittle star can change
color. It goes light when it
enters brightly lit water to
make itself harder to see.

FIVE STAR
Brittle stars have five legs—
or tentacles—and in some
species these legs are found
in a tangled mess.

EYES EVERYWHERE
There are thousands of tiny
crystal lenses covering the body
of a brittle star. They work
together as a single eye, telling
the animal if the shadow of a
predator is moving across it.

Oh look, it's a starfish! Wrong. This is a brittle star, a close relative of a starfish, and also related to spiny sea urchins and sea cucumbers. In fact, brittle stars and their relatives are the micromonsters most closely related to us. Humans and other mammals belong to a group of animals called the vertebrates—we all have a skeleton and backbone. Our bones evolved millions of years ago from an animal with the same kinds of tough plates that cover brittle stars today. Thankfully humans have developed since then. Otherwise we would live like brittle stars, scraping the weedy scum off of pebbles and rocks.

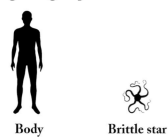

Body   **Brittle star**

SIZE COMPARISON

▶ UNLIKE STARFISH, brittle stars can walk on their five legs, lifting their central bodies off the ground. Their long legs earn these animals another name, which is serpent stars.

Five-Legged and Fast

It is easy to spot the difference between a starfish and brittle star. Brittle stars have longer legs and move around much more quickly. Starfish can also have anywhere between five and 60 tentacles, while brittle stars generally stick to five. While brittle stars scuttle across the seabed, starfish move much more slowly, using an array of piston-like tube feet that line the underside of the body.

Did you know?

• Brittle stars are a fun addition to a fish tank. Unlike a starfish, they won't kill the other creatures living there, and they move around a lot more.

• Brittle stars do not have a mouth or rear opening—they have a single central entrance for both of those jobs.

Caddisfly

Oxyethira sp

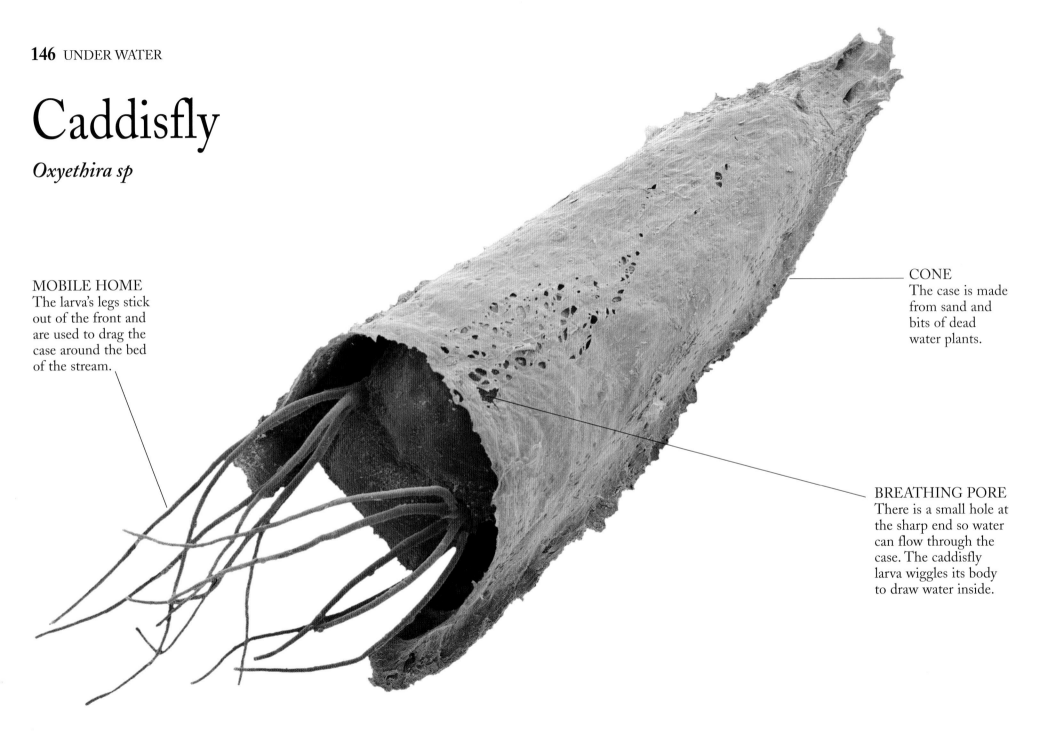

MOBILE HOME
The larva's legs stick out of the front and are used to drag the case around the bed of the stream.

CONE
The case is made from sand and bits of dead water plants.

BREATHING PORE
There is a small hole at the sharp end so water can flow through the case. The caddisfly larva wiggles its body to draw water inside.

Imagine if you had to build your own house as soon as you were born—and then carry it around on your back. That is what awaits a caddisfly larva. Begining life under water, it builds a cone-shaped case out of fragments of rotten wood, small stones, broken shells, or whatever is nearby. The case protects the larva and serves as a funnel for collecting food-filled water. When the larva is ready to change into an all-flying, air-breathing adult, it converts the case into a cocoon by blocking up the entrance. The adult then bites its way out and floats to the surface, helped by an air bubble inside the body, before flying away.

Hand   **Caddisfly**

SIZE COMPARISON

▶ AN ADULT CADDISFLY looks similar to a moth. However, their wings are hairy, not covered in scales like moths or butterflies.

Not Easily Fooled

Trout eat caddisflies as they develop from larvae into cocoons and then become adults. Anglers can trick a trout onto the hook by dangling models of the insects into the water. However, the angler must know what the real caddisflies are doing. If he or she uses the incorrect fake caddisfly for that time of year, the trout will know it is being fooled.

Did you know?

• In New Zealand, caddisflies live in the sea. Very few other insects can survive in salty water.

• Some caddisfly larvae do not build cases. Instead they knit a cone-shaped web of silk among the plant stems to collect food from the water.

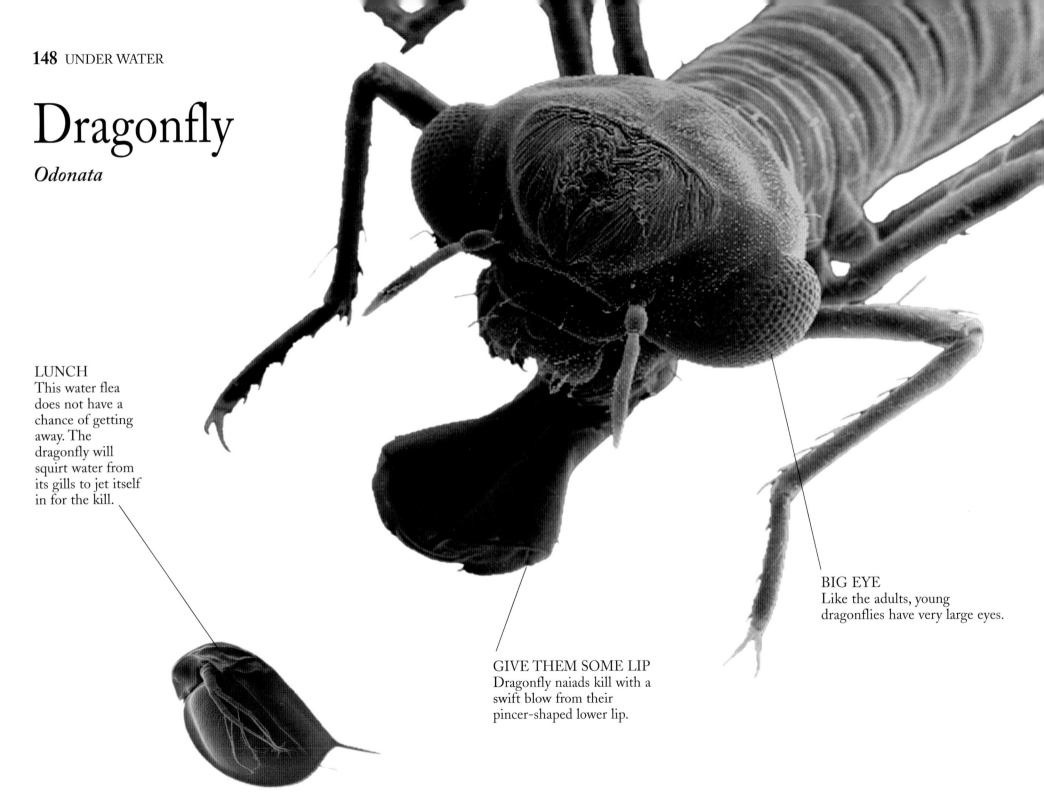

Dragonfly

Odonata

LUNCH
This water flea
does not have a
chance of getting
away. The
dragonfly will
squirt water from
its gills to jet itself
in for the kill.

GIVE THEM SOME LIP
Dragonfly naiads kill with a
swift blow from their
pincer-shaped lower lip.

BIG EYE
Like the adults, young
dragonflies have very large eyes.

The young forms of most insects are called larvae or nymphs. But baby dragonflies have a special name: naiad. The ancient Greeks believed that naiads were spirits that lived in water. They were beautiful but could also be dangerous, just like a young dragonfly. Naiads are one of the toughest hunters in streams and ponds. They prey on everything, from other water insects to tadpoles and tiny fish. In North America, some naiads crawl out of the water at night and kill spiders and beetles in the dark. Adult dragonflies are also terrifying predators. They saw up their victims with sharp teeth.

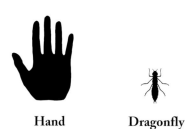

Hand   **Dragonfly**

SIZE COMPARISON

▶ A WINGED ADULT dragonfly breaks out of the dried skin of the naiad. The naiad first climbed up a plant stem to reach the air, at which point the naiad began breathing and broke out of its skin.

An Insect the Size of a Bird

Dragonflies have big wings. The largest one today has a 7¹⁄₂in (19cm) wingspan. However, dragonflies as big as gulls, with 30in (75cm) wings, flew around 250 million years ago—probably annoying the first dinosaurs. Back then, there was a lot more oxygen in the air, so insects grew much larger.

Did you know?

• Large dragonflies are called racers; smaller ones are called darters.

• Dragonflies can live for seven years in warm places. In other places, the adults are all killed by the cold of winter.

• Dragonflies are the fastest insects. Some can fly at more than 30mph (50km/h).

Great Diving Beetle

Dytiscus marginalis

SMOOTH BACK
The smooth wing case on the back shows that this beetle is a male. Females have ridges along the back.

PADDLES
The long back legs are covered in hairs, which turn them into paddles for pushing the beetle through the water.

BITERS
Diving beetles have powerful mouthparts for catching meals. They will give you a nasty bite as well.

Great diving beetles are among the largest insect you will find in the local pond. They can grow to about 1½in (4cm) long, and that makes them a match for tadpoles and minnows, their favorite foods. Both the adults and larvae are fierce hunters. That has earned them the nickname of "water tiger," though it is hard to imagine this rounded beetle as a fearsome killer. The adults float very well and it takes an effort to get themselves down deep, where all the food is. Once they have got near the bottom, they hold onto the water plants to stop themselves from popping back to the surface like a cork.

Hand

Great diving beetle

SIZE COMPARISON

▶ THIS FEMALE DIVING beetle has taken a supply of air with her under the water as bubbles trapped under the wing case. The air bubbles travel into the insect's breathing holes.

Light Seekers

Diving beetles do not spend their whole time in water. The wingless larvae crawl onto land before turning into adults. Young adults fly long distances to find new ponds. They are hard to spot in or out of water. The easiest way to find one is to drop a glow stick into a pond at night. The adult beetles and larvae are both drawn to the light.

Did you know?

• Female great diving beetles cut a slit in the stem of a water plant to lay their eggs inside.

• Diving beetles have been known to kill baby snakes.

• Male beetles have suckers on their front legs, which they use to hold onto a female during mating.

Jellyfish

Scyphozoa

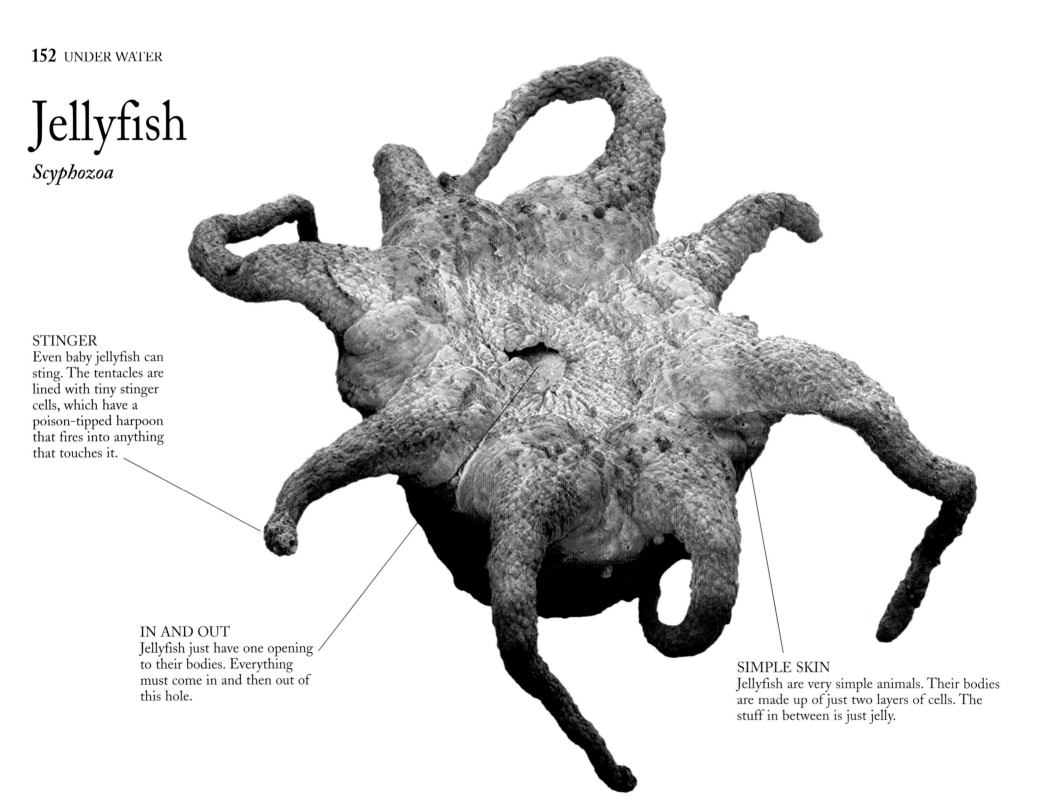

STINGER
Even baby jellyfish can sting. The tentacles are lined with tiny stinger cells, which have a poison-tipped harpoon that fires into anything that touches it.

IN AND OUT
Jellyfish just have one opening to their bodies. Everything must come in and then out of this hole.

SIMPLE SKIN
Jellyfish are very simple animals. Their bodies are made up of just two layers of cells. The stuff in between is just jelly.

A jellyfish will float on the ocean currents for months. It collects invisible particles of food, such a bacteria and algae, with its tentacles. It may feel sticky to the touch, but this sensation is caused by thousands of tiny stingers spearing the skin. Be warned, jellyfish stings can be poisonous, though most are harmless. It is hard to tell which is which, so the best advice is look but do not touch. A jellyfish has no brains—just a network of nerves, called a "nerve net." Nor does it have blood or a proper stomach. It is just a bag of jelly that collects food, so "jellybag" may be a better name than "jellyfish."

| **Full point** | **Jellyfish larvae** |
| *(100%)* | *(100%)* |

SIZE COMPARISON

▶ JELLYFISH SOMETIMES appear in huge swarms of blooms containing tens of thousands of the fish. Jellyfish can survive where many other creatures cannot, so when conditions are right, they develop in huge numbers.

Self-Illumination

Like many underwater creatures, jellyfish can make their own light. Chemicals inside their bodies makes them glow. Scientists have taken the gene for this ability and put it into mice. The result is a mouse that looks and lives like any other until you turn the light out. Then the mouse begins to glow. The jellyfish gene makes it produce the same glowing chemicals.

Did you know?

• Jellyfish are related to corals and sea anemones.

• People in China eat shredded jellyfish raw.

• The box jellyfish is one of the most venomous animals on Earth. It can kill a person in just a few minutes.

Pond Snail

Lymnaeidae

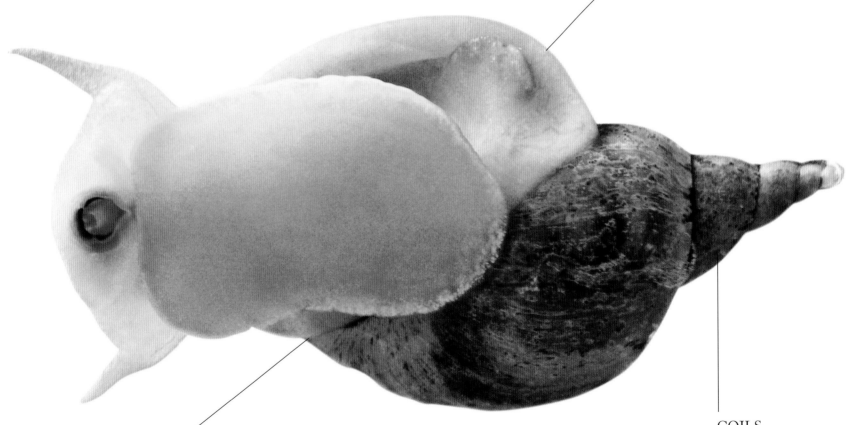

LIVING ROOM
The snail's body fits into the lower section of the shell. As the snail gets bigger, it needs to enlarge the shell.

HARD SHELL
The shell is made from calcium carbonate, the same substance in chalk.

COILS
Land snails have shells that are coiled sideways, but the shells of many water snails often coil upward.

After rain, it often seems that snails come from everywhere, sliding over garden walls and lawns. In fact, most snails hate the land—they live in water instead. The snails that live in the ocean have a number of names, from limpet and whelk to winkle and conch. The snails that live in freshwater—rivers and ponds—do not have fancy names. They are just "snails." Pond snails look a bit like their landlubber cousins. Land snails use their shells as moist dens, where they can hide out when the weather gets too hot. Pond snails do not need to worry about that, and the shell is used as a suit of armor instead.

Full point
(Magnified 5 times)

Pond snail
(Magnified 5 times)

SIZE COMPARISON

▶ A SNAIL BEGINS life with a tiny curved shell. As the shell grows, it will become a longer and heavier coil, but at this size it floats in the water as a piece of plankton.

Breathing Through its Foot

Have you ever seen a pond snail floating on its back at the surface? It is not having a rest. It is simply sticking its fleshy foot through the water to get some fresh air. It breathes with a small gill under the back of the shell. However, it can also absorb the oxygen it needs from the water straight through the skin. The snail never has to leave the water.

Did you know?

• Snail eggs form layers of jelly on the underside of the leaves of water plants.

• Pond snails eat grains of sand to grind up their food into a pulp inside the stomach.

• Snail shells nearly always coil to the right.

Ragworm

Nereis succinea

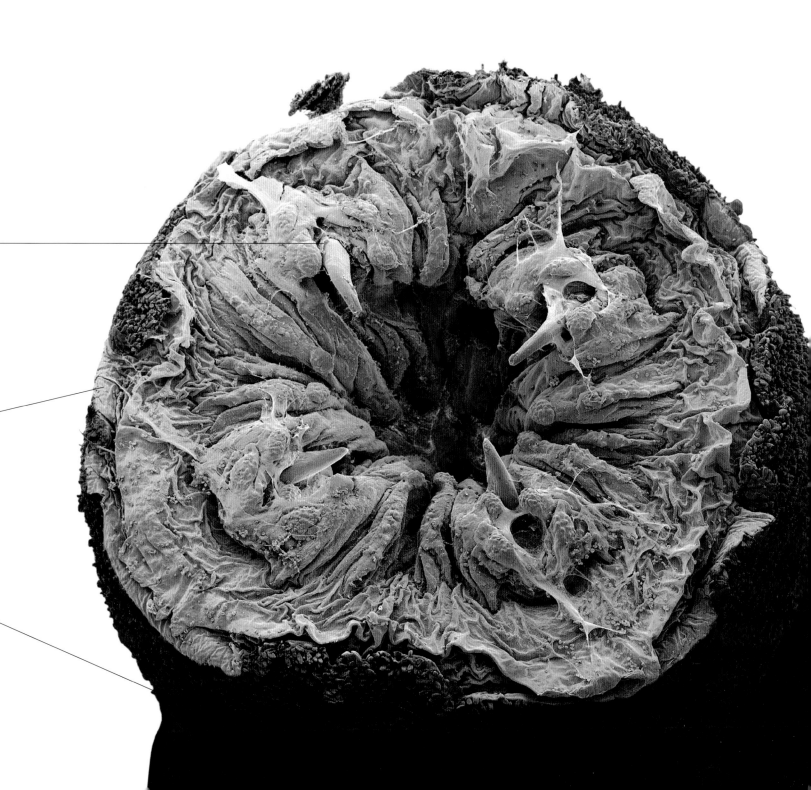

TEETH
There are four pointed
teeth around the
mouth. These are used
for spearing prey and
scraping food from
pebbles.

JAWLESS MOUTH
The worm does not have a jaw,
so the mouth does not snap
open and shut like yours.
Instead, the opening is closed by
twisting and squeezing muscles.

GOING GREEN
Ragworms are red-brown
most of the time, but they
go green during the
breeding season.

Buried under rocks or deep inside the soggy mud of a river mouth, the ragworm is a fierce predator. This frilled wriggler has sharp teeth, which shoot out rapidly to grasp other soft-bodied animals. However, the ragworm does not rely on hunting alone. It will burrow through the mud, looking for animals that are already dead, and is happy to graze on seaweeds as well. The worm also fishes for food. It weaves a silk net at the entrance to the burrow. This net collects tiny bits of food as the worm draws water through it by wriggling its body. When the net is full, the worm eats it up, silk and all.

Hand

Ragworm

SIZE COMPARISON

▶ RAGWORMS ARE A type of bristleworm. The bristles—or chaetae—are used to help the worm wriggle along. They also work as gills, collecting oxygen from the water around the worm.

Living by the Moon

The lives of ragworms are controlled by the moon. Every female worm times her eggs to be ready by a certain phase of the moon. (Whether it is a new moon or full moon depends on where the worm lives.) When the time is right, the female's body becomes stiff, and the eggs burst out of her—along with the rest of her insides. Smelly chemicals lure the males to the eggs, and they fertilize them so they will grow into new worms. Then the adult males also die.

Did you know?

• Ever wondered what flocks of shorebirds are so busy looking for? Ragworms are top of their list.

• The hard material in ragworm teeth is so light and yet so strong that it might be used to build aircraft in future.

• Ragworms make good bait for fishing.

Sea Urchin

Echinoidea

STOMACH SAC
The mouth is at the center of the body and it connects to a baglike stomach, which can be seen through the thin skin.

FOOD TRAPS
The baby sea urchin has eight tentacles, or arms (not all seen), that it uses to collect food. These are covered in tiny hairs that waft the food into the mouth.

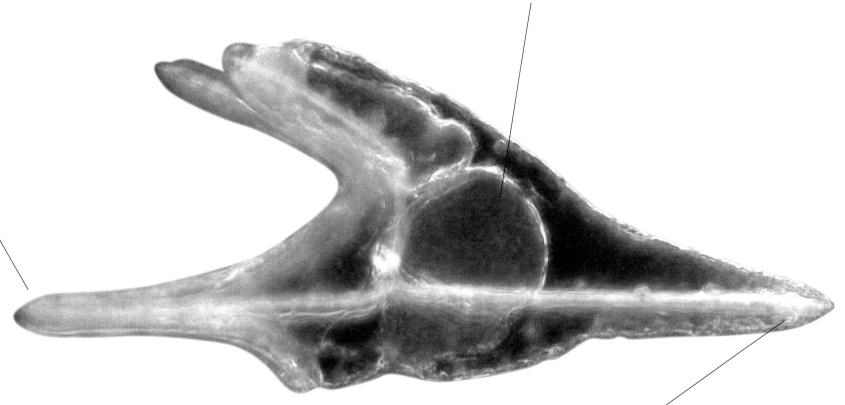

CONE SHAPE
The urchin larva is not round, it is more like a cone. The bottom is at the pointed end.

Sea urchins are covered in hard spines made from chalky minerals. If you tread on an urchin, their spines will spear your foot. Their tips may then break off inside the wound, and will hurt badly if you do not get them out. However, even the spiniest urchins began life as tiny swimming blobs of jelly floating in the water. As they grow, the sea urchins begin to harden and eventually they sink to the bottom, setting up home among the seaweeds. It may seem surprising, but adult urchins walk around looking for fresh food—most eat seaweeds. They just move so slowly you cannot tell that they are moving.

Full point
(Magnified 20 times)

Sea urchin
(Magnified 20 times)

SIZE COMPARISON

▶ AN ADULT SEA urchin body develops from the cone-shaped baby into a rounded shape. It is divided into five sections, all surrounding the central mouth. In a sense, they are like starfish but without the arms or tentacles.

A Split Stomach

Each of the urchin's five body sections provide a single tooth, which work together to gnaw away at the stems of seaweeds. From the mouth the stomach splits into five sections, but they join back together to form a single exit. The Greek thinker Aristotle was the first person to describe the urchin's guts. The round toothy mouth is now remembered as the "Aristotle lantern" in his memory.

Did you know?

• Red sea urchins from the Pacific Ocean can live for more than 200 years—although most make it to about 30.

• The word "urchin" comes from the Old English word for "hedgehog."

• Sea urchin eggs are sometimes spread on toast in the Orkneys.

Water Bear

Echiniscus sp

BODY PLAN
Adult water bears of the same species always have exactly the same number of body cells.

STUMPS
Tardigrades have four body segments (plus the head) and each segment has a pair of legs. However, the legs do not have any joints so they are not good for walking.

DOUBLE CLAWS
Each foot has at least four claws. Some species have as many as eight.

Water bear is a cute name used for a member of a strange group of animals called the tardigrades. "Tardigrade" itself means "slow walker," and these minute creatures apparently walk the way bears do, hence their name. You won't have seen one before. They grow to only about ¹⁄₁₀mm long, while a newly hatched larva may be half that size. The first person to see one had to use a microscope. Despite their name, water bears are not only found in muddy puddles and in damp soil. They are also found high up mountains, under ice, in sand dunes, and even on the seabed.

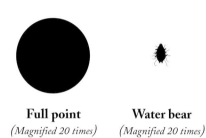

Full point
(Magnified 20 times)

Water bear
(Magnified 20 times)

SIZE COMPARISON

▶ TARDIGRADES HAVE sharp mouthparts that are used to suck the liquid from plants and other soft food, including tiny worms.

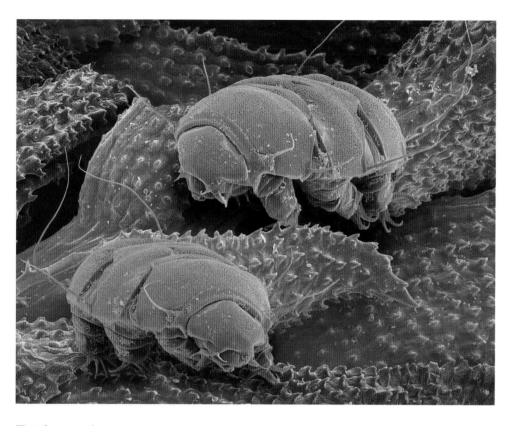

Hardy Survivors

Tardigrades can breathe only in wet places. If they dry out, the animals form tough barrel-shaped cysts that can survive just about anything. Some have been frozen to the lowest temperatures possible—and lived. Others have been heated to 300°F (150°C) and blasted with radiation that would make a human sizzle. The water bears were fine once they were covered in water again.

Did you know?

• Tardigrades are also known as moss piglets.

• Water bear cysts were taken into orbit in 2007 and left in the vacuum of space for 10 days. And most of them survived the journey home.

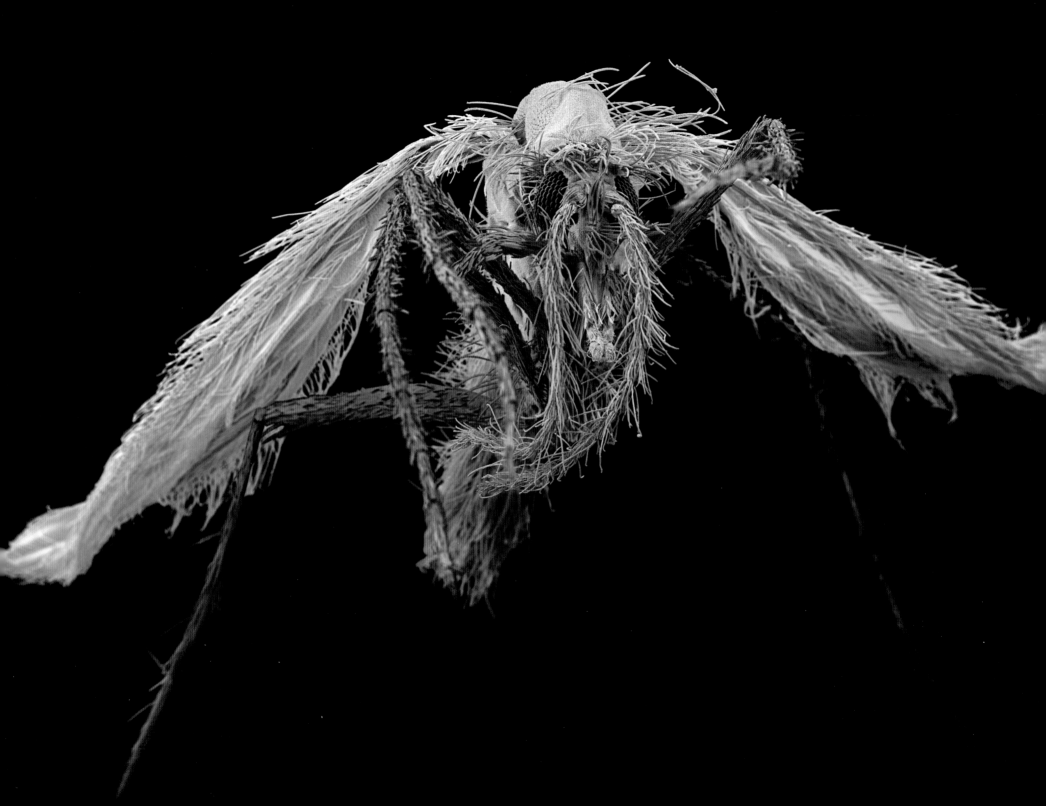

In the Danger Zone

B E AFRAID. Be very afraid. These micromonsters can be deadly—or at the very least they are a warning that a lot of trouble is on the way. Many biting micromonsters do more than cause annoying itches—they can give you a killer disease. They may look no different from other pesty nippers and suckers but it is what's on the inside that counts. The little monsters are filled with bacteria and viruses, which are harmless to them, but will make us very ill.

You could say that the deadly bugs spread those diseases by accident. But other micromonsters will think nothing of killing you. They have super-powerful venom that is meant to do away with much smaller creatures. But it is so strong it can kill an fully grown adult in minutes. These venomous monsters are not snakes or scorpions, they are much worse—a snail and a spiderlike tick that is almost too small to see!

To those who know, these bugs are much scarier and deadlier than even the biggest and fiercest hunters on Earth. Will you recognize one when you see it?

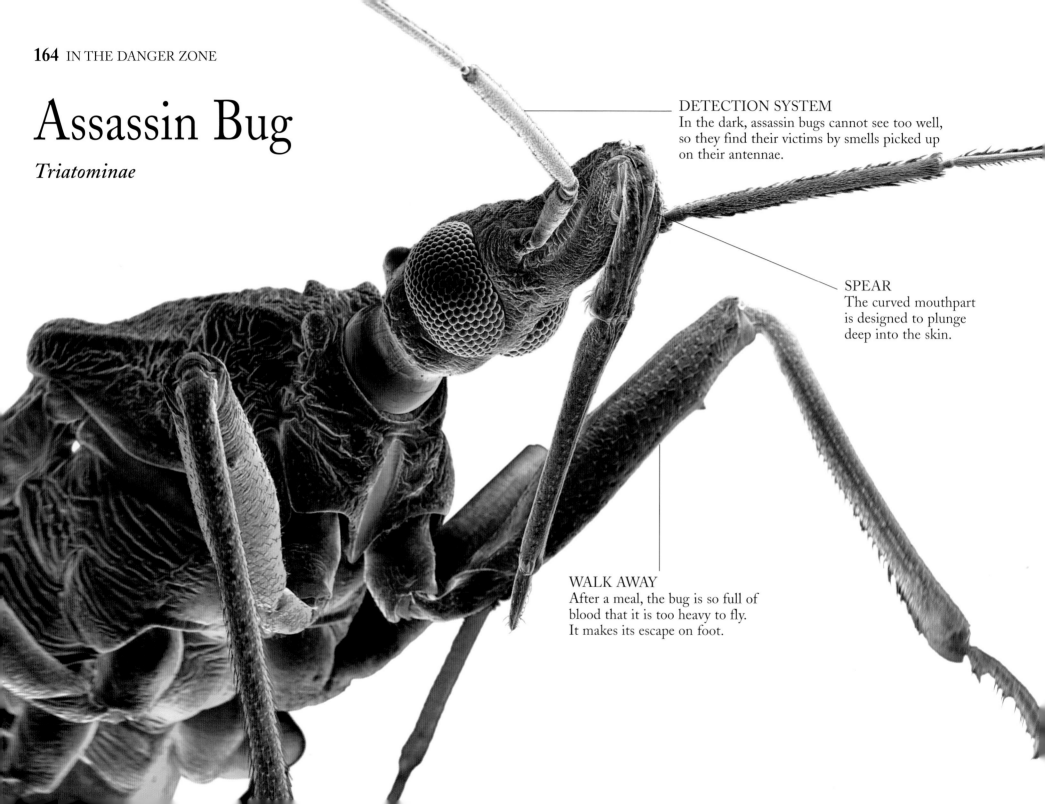

Assassin Bug

Triatominae

DETECTION SYSTEM
In the dark, assassin bugs cannot see too well, so they find their victims by smells picked up on their antennae.

SPEAR
The curved mouthpart is designed to plunge deep into the skin.

WALK AWAY
After a meal, the bug is so full of blood that it is too heavy to fly. It makes its escape on foot.

Assassin bugs hunt alone. The South American insects arrive unseen in the darkness. They time their attacks for when their victims are asleep and powerless to resist. By the time a victim has even realized he or she has been attacked, the bug has disappeared. But the damage has been done—and could cause death! The assassin bug uses its fearsome spike of a mouth to suck blood. It also leaves a sprinkle of droppings. When you wake up and rub the itchy bite, germs from the droppings are spread into your blood. The germs causes an illness called Chagas' disease, which kills sufferers slowly over many years.

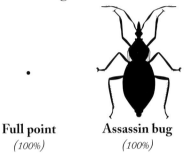

Full point
(100%)

Assassin bug
(100%)

SIZE COMPARISON

▶ NOT ALL ASSASSIN bugs suck human blood. Other types, such as the wheel bug, stalk insects, killing them with their sharp mouths. The wheel bug is named after the cog-shaped ridge on its back.

Kiss of Death

Assassin bugs that attack humans and spread Chagas' disease are also known as kissing bugs. This second name comes from their habit of sucking blood from the soft skin around the lips. The bugs also target the skin around the eyes. Kissing bugs are also an ingredient in Mexican love potions, but they probably do more harm than good because they are another source of Chagas' disease.

Did you know?

• Charles Darwin caught Chagas' disease in 1835, when he was studying the animals and plants of South America. Darwin's work in America helped him to figure out his Theory of Evolution.

• In Central America, the droppings of assassin bugs are used as a traditional medicine for warts.

• Some 20,000 people die from Chagas' disease every year.

Blackfly

Simulium

CLUBBED ANTENNAE
The blackfly's stout, cigar-shaped antennae are much bigger than the antennae of most flies.

FEMALE EYE
Blackflies have very large eyes. It is easy to tell this one is a female because her eyes do not touch, as the eyes of a male do.

HUMPBACKS
Adult blackflies have an armored plate on the back, which gives them the look of a hunchback.

Blackflies are bloodsuckers that live in most parts of the world. Most are harmless to people—although their bites can create a painful pimple. However, the bites of some blackflies in Central America and Africa cause much more suffering. All blackflies spend their early lives in lakes and rivers, and they spread river blindness. The disease is caused by tiny worms that pass into a person's blood from the fly when it bites. These breed inside the body, causing swellings and itchy skin. Dead worms eventually spread to the eyes, making a victim go blind. At least 17 million people suffer from river blindness.

Full point
(Magnified 2 times)

Blackfly
(Magnified 2 times)

SIZE COMPARISON

▶ THE BLACKFLY LARVAE live under water. They do not swim but attach themselves to rocks and sift food from the water using a rakelike fan on their heads.

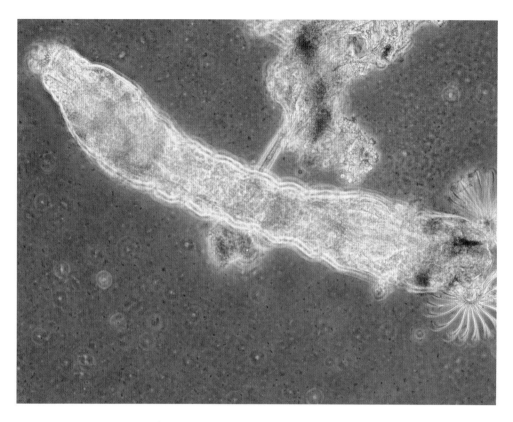

Female Bloodsuckers

Like many biting insects, it is only the female blackflies that suck blood. The rich food enables them to grow eggs, which are laid on the stem of a water plant. Once hatched, the blackfly larvae dive into the water, where they filter food from the water. After growing large enough, the larvae then become pupae, and evolve into an adult. The new adult is not a water animal, so it rides to the surface in a bubble of air.

Did you know?

• River blindness can be cured by taking two pills every three years. However, everyone in the problem areas needs to take it at the same time.

• It takes years for the worms to make a person blind. In places where river blindness is worst, children have to lead the blind adults around, because the children are still young enough to see.

Cone Shell

Conus sp

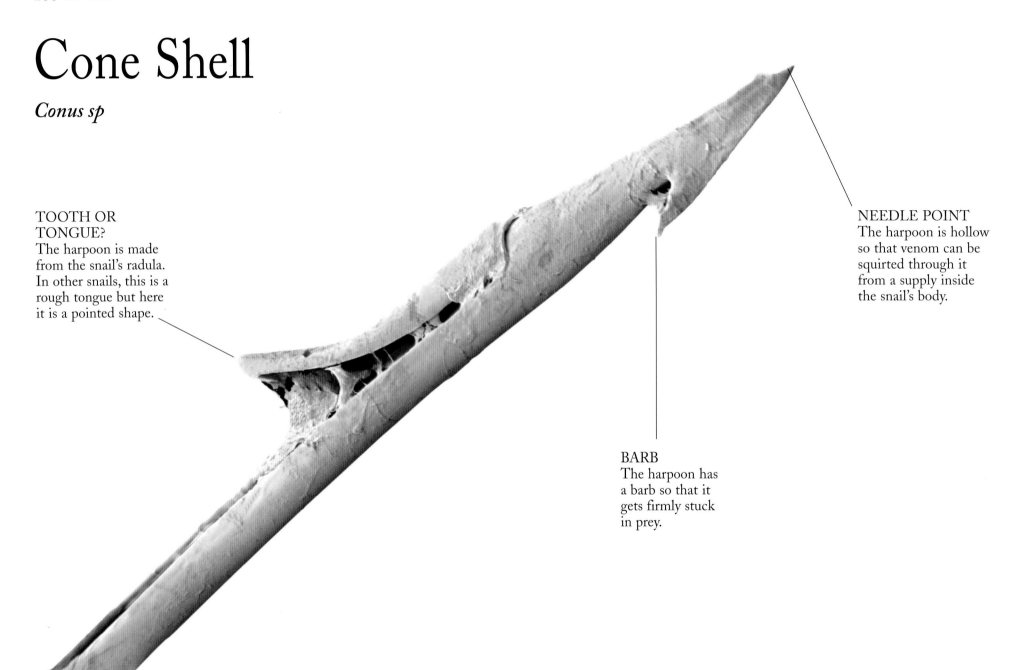

TOOTH OR TONGUE?
The harpoon is made from the snail's radula. In other snails, this is a rough tongue but here it is a pointed shape.

NEEDLE POINT
The harpoon is hollow so that venom can be squirted through it from a supply inside the snail's body.

BARB
The harpoon has a barb so that it gets firmly stuck in prey.

Not all snails are gentle vegetarians. The sea snails known as cone shells are quite the opposite! They harpoon their prey with a poison dart tipped with some of the deadliest venom in the natural world. Smaller cone shells prey on worms, while large ones go for fish. Some of the bigger cone shells are dangerous to humans.

Although they release just small amounts of venom in each sting, it can be enough to kill. Their harpoon tongues can slice through gloves and even wetsuits. Divers who get stung by the most dangerous snails, which live in the Indian Ocean, may have just minutes to live!

Hand

Cone shell

SIZE COMPARISON

▶ THE CONE SHELL prepares to fire the harpoon by extending a long trunk, or proboscis. The mouth is at the end and there are tiny eye stalks on either side of it. Once the harpoon has fired, the mouth opens very wide to eat the prey.

Dangerous Research

Doctors are studying the venom of cone shells to see if it could be used for medicines. However, to study it they need to milk the deadly snails. If an accident happens, there is no cure the doctor can take. Instead he or she must be rushed to hospital and kept alive by a machine, until the snail poison has stopped working.

Did you know?

• The geography cone shell has dark blotches on its shell, which make it look like a map. It is the most common and feared cone shell.

• Some of the chemicals in cone shell venom are painkillers. One of them may prove to be the strongest painkiller ever found.

Fire-Detecting Beetle

Melanophila acuminata

METALLIC
The fire-detecting beetles are also called Jewel Beetles because their backs shimmer like polished metal or the surface of a CD.

FIRE ALARM
The beetles can detect the heat from the fire using sensitive plates behind the middle legs.

BITERS
Fire-detecting beetles give nasty bites if you get in the way and come between them and the fire.

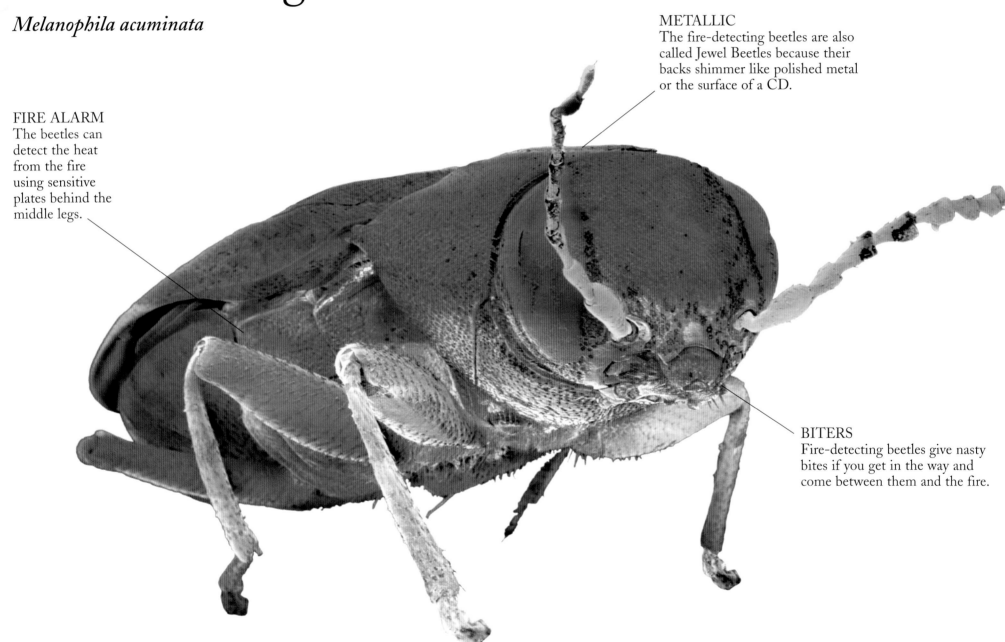

If you see one of these insects flying past, run in the other direction! A forest fire is on its way. Firefighters tackling wild fires often report a swarm of insects flying into the smoldering remains of the forest. Some have come to raid the nests of insects that lived under the bark before the fire—and now have no protection. The fire-detecting beetle is looking for freshly burned trees. It lays its eggs on the charred logs, and the grubs burrow into the wood underneath. A living tree would kill the beetle grubs with gooey resins or squash them as they grow. But thanks to forest fires, the beetles have plenty of easy food.

Hand

Fire-detecting beetle

SIZE COMPARISON

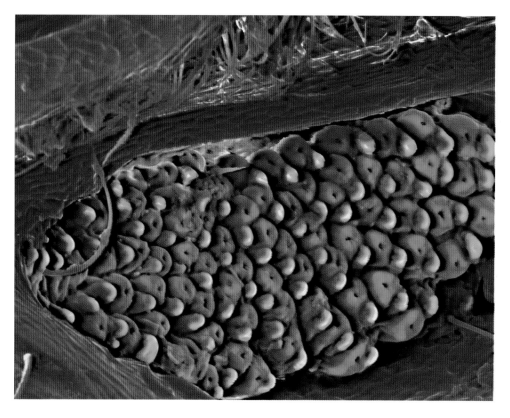

▶ THE HEAT-SENSITIVE PLATES can pick up fires from more than 7 miles (12km) away. Scientists are trying to figure out how they work so well. One day, something like the beetle's fire sensor could be used in our own fire alarms or heat-sensitive cameras.

Growing from the Ashes

A forest fire is terrifying if you are caught in its path. The flames can travel much faster than people can run and the heat could turn them to ash in the blink of an eye. However, many forests needs fires from time to time. The flames clear out the dead wood, making way for young trees. The ash makes the soil fertile again, and some plant seeds will sprout only once they have been toasted by a flame.

Did you know?

- Jewel beetle larvae can survive inside a dead tree trunk for 30 years.

- Pit vipers and pythons can also "see" things by the heat they give off.

- The fire-detecting beetles can smell smoke from more than 30 miles (50km) away.

Locust

Orthoptera

HOPPER
A locust swarm begins on foot. Wingless nymphs called hoppers bound around getting more and more agitated before changing into fast-flying adults.

SHORT HORNS
Locusts are a type of short-horned grasshopper. The horns in question are the insect's antennae.

BUILT FOR SWARMING
The form of the swarming locust is darker than the green, resting insect. It is also longer and broader to carry large wings for flying for days on end.

Normally, locusts are simple grasshoppers. But with little warning, they can form into a swarm of billions. A locust swarm can block out the sun, and consume a field of crops in minutes. The problem starts if the grasshoppers get so overcrowded that they rub against each other. This releases chemicals in the locust's brain, which makes the next batch of eggs grow into swarming locusts. These set off to find more space. If they don't, the crowd of locusts keeps growing into a swarm that can travel across continents for months. It breaks up only once the insects have found enough food for all.

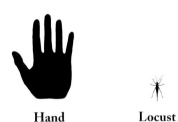

Hand   **Locust**

SIZE COMPARISON

▶ MOST SWARMS ATTACK dry parts of Africa and the Middle East. They can cover more than 60 miles (100km) in a single day, devastating crops as they go.

Did you know?

• In 1988, a locust swarm from Africa flew across the Atlantic Ocean and attacked the Caribbean islands.

• Each locust eats more than $\frac{1}{16}$oz (2g) of food a day. So a billion-strong swarm gets through 220 tons (200 metric tonnes)!

Saved by Seagulls

Crickets are not the same as grasshoppers. The easiest way to spot the difference is the antennae. A cricket has long ones that stretch behind the body. Some crickets swarm in the same ways as their cousins. The first Mormons to settle in Utah in the 1840s were in danger of starving because crickets ate their wheat. However, the settlers were saved by a huge flock of seagulls from the California coast, which ate the cricket swarm.

Lyme Disease Tick

Ixodes ricinus

LITTLE LEGS
The legs are too short for walking after a meal. The tick falls to the ground and lies there, digesting.

JUST SWELL
The tick sucks blood for several days and swells up to 20 times its original size.

I magine an animal with a mouth like a chainsaw and a stomach like a balloon. This is a tick, a relative of spiders and scorpions. Similar to the mite, it has a single rounded body section and eight stubby legs but is much bigger: Some grow longer than $1/16$in (2mm)! All ticks are bloodsuckers and they must wait for a meal until an animal brushes past, perhaps for years. The tick needs only three meals—one as a larva, one as a nymph, and the last as an adult. As it feeds, however, it spreads bacteria of several diseases. One of them is Lyme disease, which causes rashes and chills but may then attack the heart and brain.

Full point
(Magnified 20 times)

Lyme disease tick
(Magnified 20 times)

SIZE COMPARISON

▶ A TICK SAWS into the skin using a spike covered in teeth. The blood is sucked up through a tube running down the middle of the spike.

A Recent Infection

Lyme disease is a new disease. It emerged only in the late 1970s, and it is a growing problem in North America. Places with a lot of wild deer will be Lyme disease hotspots. Ticks spread many other diseases too, including typhus and Rocky Mountain spotted fever.

Did you know?

• Tick larvae have only six legs when they hatch from the egg. They grow an extra pair as they get older.

• Typhus becomes a problem during wars when people live close together and do not have the chance to wash their tick-covered clothes very often.

Malaria Mosquito

Anopheles sp

FRILLED ANTENNAE
The mosquito flies in the dark and homes in on human victims by picking up the gases in their breath.

BLOOD STRAW
The mosquito bites using a long, sharp proboscis. This is flanked by two hairy feelers, or palps.

ROOM FOR MORE
Only a female mosquito sucks blood. Her abdomen will swell up with the blood.

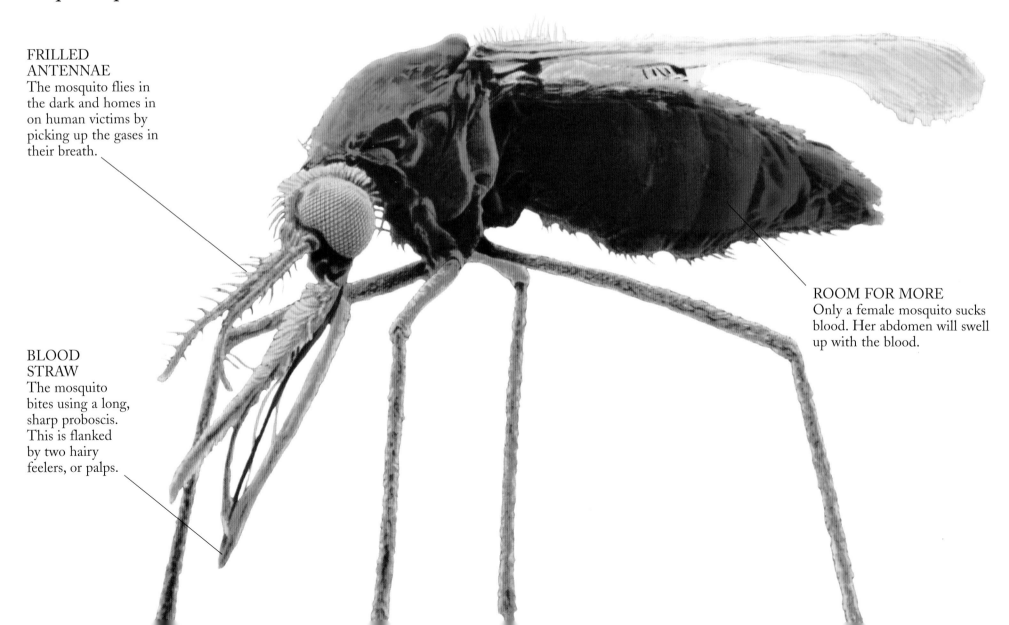

What is the most dangerous animal on Earth? The grizzly bear? The crocodile? You need to look for something much smaller and sneakier—the *Anopheles* mosquito. A bite from this tiny insect could give a person malaria, the most dangerous disease in the world. The disease is caused by a tiny germ that hides out in the mosquito's salivary glands. Before the little fly sucks the blood of a human, it first squirts in a little bit of saliva, and the malaria germs surge into the blood supply. There are up to 500 million people affected by malaria each year, and every year between one and three million die of it.

Full point
(Magnified 3 times)

Malaria mosquito
(Magnified 3 times)

SIZE COMPARISON

▶ THE SIMPLEST WAY of avoiding malaria is to sleep under a mosquito net. Malaria mosquitoes fly mostly after dark, so you can stay safe under a fine net. Even a small mosquito cannot get through the holes.

A Menace in Africa

You can catch malaria in most warm parts of the world. However, 90 percent of the people who suffer from malaria come from Africa, and most of the people who die are young children. The reason for this is because African people cannot buy enough nets, and it is hard for them to get hold of medicines.

Did you know?

• Mosquito larvae live in smelly, stagnant water.

• The little insects makes a whine as they flap their wings.

• A vaccine against malaria is currently being tested.

Paralysis Tick

Rhipicephalus sanguineus

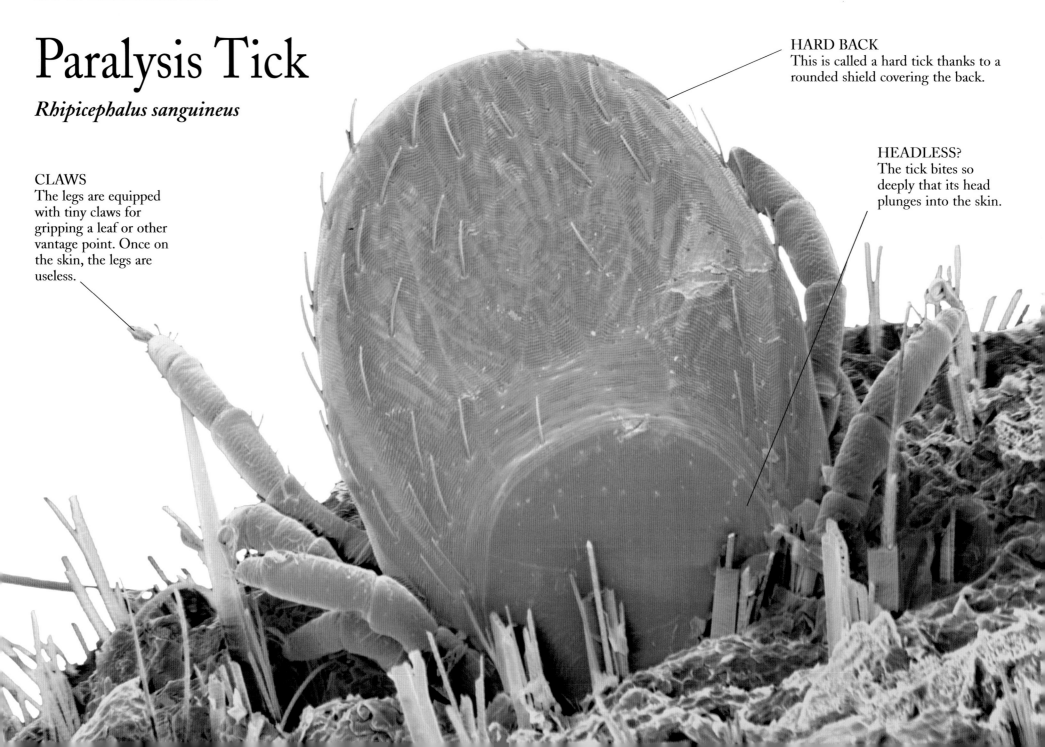

HARD BACK
This is called a hard tick thanks to a rounded shield covering the back.

HEADLESS?
The tick bites so deeply that its head plunges into the skin.

CLAWS
The legs are equipped with tiny claws for gripping a leaf or other vantage point. Once on the skin, the legs are useless.

Ticks spread several diseases by pumping germs into our blood. However, the paralysis tick is the only one that lays us low all by itself. This Australian tick's saliva contains a tiny amount of poison. At first, a tick bite does not have any effect. But after several days, the tick is still there, and the poisons begin to work. Victims—whether livestock, dogs, or people—begin to feel weak and become unsteady on their legs. Within hours, they may be completely paralyzed. That is extremely dangerous because the heart muscles stop working! Fortunately, doctors normally remove the tick before that happens.

Full point
(Magnified 10 times)

Paralysis tick
(Magnified 10 times)

SIZE COMPARISON

▶ A MALE TICK is much smaller than the female. He does not suck blood himself. During mating, he bites open the blood-filled body of the female and slurps up the food.

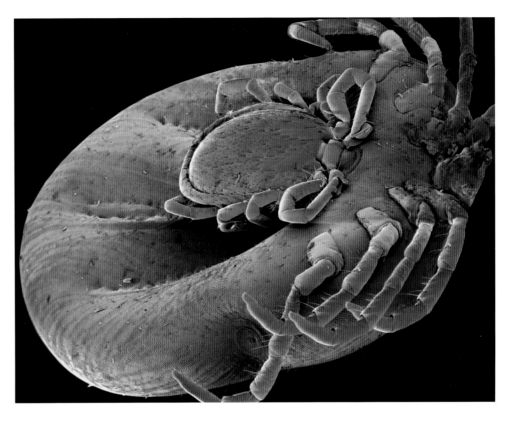

Off to the Vet

Tick paralysis is most common in Australia, although it can also happen in other parts of the world. Only a handful of people are killed by the ticks—fewer than one a year. However, farm animals and pets do get attacked. Each year, about 10,000 dogs have to be taken to a vet to have a tick removed.

Did you know?

• Paralysis can be caused by 43 different types of tick.

• Ticks must be removed carefully, or their jaws and head may be ripped off and stay stuck in the skin.

Sandfly

Phlebotomos sp

DARK EYES
Sandflies have
particularly large
dark eyes.

SCISSOR MOUTH
Only females suck blood.
They use their mouths as
shears to slice into the skin.

HAIRY SUCKER
Sandflies are very
hairy. There are hairs
all over the antennae,
mouthparts, and
even the wings.

Sandflies are small bloodsuckers. They are most common in the dry parts of Europe and Asia and the great deserts of North Africa—hence the name sandfly. However, sandflies are also common in the jungles of South America. They spread diseases as they bite and are responsible for giving people three illnesses. Pappataci fever is common in southern Europe and the Middle East, and normally cures itself. Carrion's disease produces large warts all over the body. But the worst disease is leishmaniasis. This creates sores on the skin and sometime inside the body, too. It kills about 60,000 people every year.

Full point
(*Magnified 7 times*)

Sandfly
(*Magnified 7 times*)

SIZE COMPARISON

▶ MOST INSECTS EITHER lay their wings flat or hold them upright when they are not flying. Sandflies do it differently. They rest their wings in a tell-tale V-shape as they prepare to give you a bite.

Black Fever

Leishmaniasis, or black fever, is one of the world's worst tropical diseases. About 12 million people live with the illness and hundreds of thousands catch it every year. Most cases are seen in India and Laos, where it kills many thousands every year. The disease can be treated by a course of strong drugs that drive the wormlike bug from the body.

Did you know?

• South American sandflies live in the roosts of bats. The bats also have the leishmaniasis bug in their blood, but it does not make them sick.

• Pappataci fever is a common childhood disease. The name *pappataci* comes from the Italian word for sandfly.

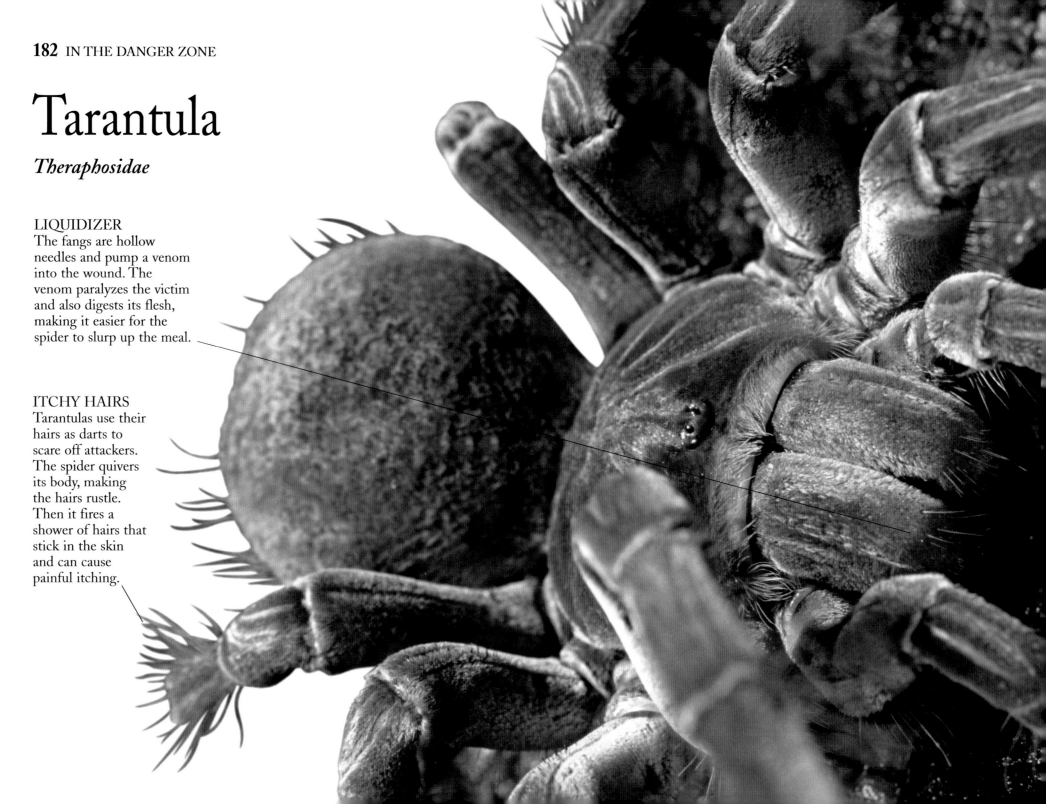

Tarantula

Theraphosidae

LIQUIDIZER
The fangs are hollow needles and pump a venom into the wound. The venom paralyzes the victim and also digests its flesh, making it easier for the spider to slurp up the meal.

ITCHY HAIRS
Tarantulas use their hairs as darts to scare off attackers. The spider quivers its body, making the hairs rustle. Then it fires a shower of hairs that stick in the skin and can cause painful itching.

Tarantulas certainly look dangerous. They are huge—the largest would straddle a dinner plate! They also have two long fangs dripping with venom. So surely these are the top killers of the spider world? Thankfully, these furry bundles of fun are pretty harmless. Their bites can be painful but are normally no more dangerous than a wasp sting. The biggest spiders may attack a mouse or bird but they have no interest in people. If you come across a tarantula, it will be able to see you with at least one of its eight eyes. The spider then rears up on its back legs, showing off its fangs as a warning: "Don't come any closer!"

Hand

Tarantula

SIZE COMPARISON

▶ TARANTULAS AMBUSH THEIR victims at high speed. This one is after a snake. The spider lays out a series of silk trip wires around its den, which work as an early-warning system that some prey is coming its way.

What's in a Name?

The name "tarantula" has a long history. The original tarantula spider lived in Italy, but was actually a type of wolf spider. Local people thought a bite from this spider would create a frenzied attack of twitching—a bit like a dance called the tarantella. When European explorers reached the Americas, they found big and hairy spiders, which they named tarantulas. The name has stuck, although Asian and African tarantulas are also known as baboon spiders.

Did you know?

• It takes 12 years for a baby tarantula to become an adult.

• Human red blood cells carry oxygen using an iron-rich chemical. Tarantula blood is very unusual because it uses copper chemicals instead.

• The Texas brown tarantula builds a sticky silk net for hauling soil away as it digs its den.

Tiger Mosquito
Aedes albopictus

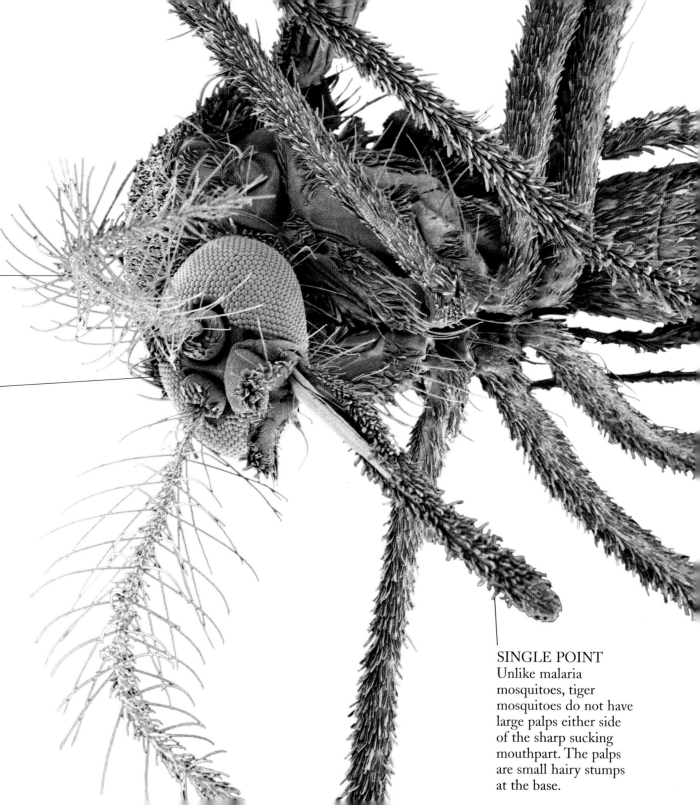

LISTEN EAR
The antennae are covered in hairy plumes. These are used to pick up smells and can also hear the whine of other mosquitoes flying nearby.

EYE IN THE SKY
Tiger mosquitoes do not wait until dusk to attack. They bite during the day, unlike other mosquitoes. They use their big eyes to track the next victim.

SINGLE POINT
Unlike malaria mosquitoes, tiger mosquitoes do not have large palps either side of the sharp sucking mouthpart. The palps are small hairy stumps at the base.

As you might expect, a tiger mosquito has stripes. It comes from Southeast Asia, but it has become quite a world traveler in recent years and has spread to several new places. In Southeast Asia, the mosquitoes spread dengue fever. The aches and pains are so bad that sufferers think they have broken bones! And they will die without treatment. Tiger mosquitoes also spread West Nile virus, which attacks the brain. Tiger mosquitoes are thought to have introduced this killer disease to North America in 1999. No one is quite sure how they got there. They may have traveled aboard a passenger jet.

Full point	Tiger mosquito
(100%)	*(100%)*

SIZE COMPARISON

▶ TIGER MOSQUITOS SPEND the first part of their lives in water. The tiny larvae hang upside down from the surface of the water. Diseases spread by mosquitos are most common in swampy places, where there is plenty of still water. Mosquitos do not like streams and rivers much.

Attracted to Sweat

How do you trap a tiger mosquito? By luring it with the same things that attract it to humans in the first place. That means putting a source of carbon dioxide in the bait. We breathe out this gas, and it is one of the first things a mosquito looks for. The other ingredients are a little less appetizing—the chemicals that make our armpits smell! These are acids and oils produced from our sweat. They smell bad to us but are delicious to a hungry tiger mosquito.

Did you know?

• Tiger mosquitoes also spread heartworms to dogs and cats.

• In 2006, tiger mosquitoes spread a fever to a third of the population of the island of La Réunion in the Indian Ocean. In total, a quarter of a million people were affected, and 250 died.

Tsetse Fly

Glossina sp

FEEDING BULB
Tsetse flies look similar to common houseflies. However, they have long mouthparts that join onto a bulb-shaped structure under the head.

NEAT WINGS
Tsetse flies fold their wings so that one lies right on top of the other as they rest over the back. Most other flies have their wings spread out a little.

BLOOD TUBE
Both male and female tsetses have knifelike mouthparts that cut into the skin for drinking blood.

The word "tsetse" is pronounced *t'setsee*. The name may be difficult to say, but you will not forget the tsetse. After the malaria mosquito, it is the deadliest African fly around. Both the male and female tsetse flies suck blood. They prey on large mammals, such as antelopes and horses, but they also attack humans. The flies spread the same kind of disease to all its hosts. Animals are struck down by an illness called nagana, but the human form is sleeping sickness. This attacks the nerves, making sufferers feel so weak that they eventually seem to be asleep. One quarter of a million people die of it each year.

Full point
(100%)

Tsetse fly
(100%)

SIZE COMPARISON

▶ SLEEPING SICKNESS is caused by single-celled parasites called trypanosomes. The disease is so hard to beat because the trypanosomes are good at disguising themselves. They frequently change the chemicals on their surface, which makes them invisible to the body's defenses.

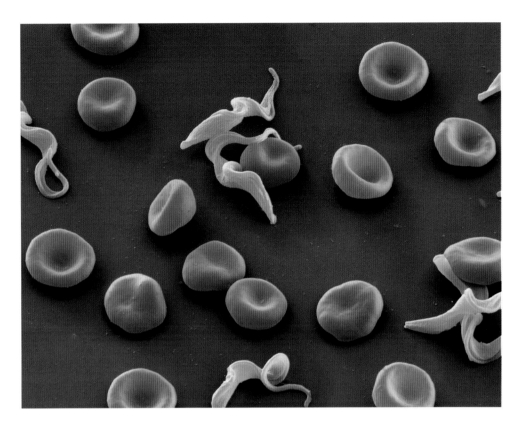

Doting Mother

Tsetse flies make very good parents. They are one of very few insects that produce only one egg at a time. The egg hatches inside the mother, and it stays there as she feeds her young on milky food. The larva is born only when it is fully grown—almost the size of the mother. As soon as it leaves the mother's body, the larva transforms into a fully formed adult. Now you can understand why the mother needs to drink so much blood.

Did you know?

• Sleeping sickness is similar to Chagas' disease, which is spread by assassin bugs.

• Tsetse fly traps are electric blue because the flies seem most attracted to that color.

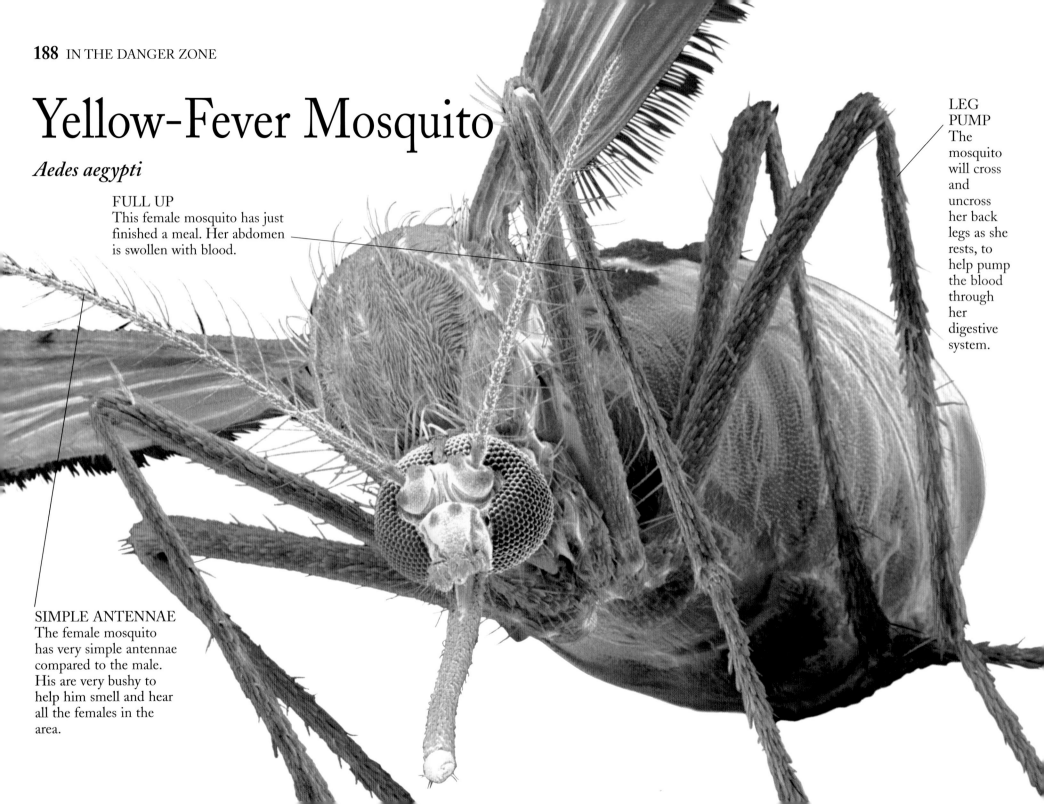

Yellow-Fever Mosquito

Aedes aegypti

FULL UP
This female mosquito has just finished a meal. Her abdomen is swollen with blood.

LEG PUMP
The mosquito will cross and uncross her back legs as she rests, to help pump the blood through her digestive system.

SIMPLE ANTENNAE
The female mosquito has very simple antennae compared to the male. His are very bushy to help him smell and hear all the females in the area.

Yellow fever is caused by a virus. The virus has several horrible effects, but when it attacks the liver it makes a sufferer's skin go yellow. The disease is spread by a mosquito called *Aedes aegypti*. This mosquito lives in many warm parts of the world, but it spreads yellow fever only in Central Africa and parts of South America. There is a vaccine against yellow fever and in most countries the disease is quite rare. Using mosquito nets to avoid getting bitten is the best line of defense. However, in the poorest African countries, yellow fever is still a big killer. About 30,000 people die from the disease every year.

Full point
(*Magnified 3 times*)

Yellow-fever mosquito
(*Magnified 3 times*)

SIZE COMPARISON

▶ YELLOW-FEVER MOSQUITOES are said to have the shape of a lyre on their backs. That is useful to know only if it is sitting still enough to see— perhaps as it bites you—and you know what a lyre looks like! A lyre is an old-fashioned harp with the strings running up from a rounded base. Can you see it?

Black Vomit

Yellow fever is an African disease but was brought to the Americas by mosquitoes on board a ship—probably one carrying African slaves. The disease roared through Mexico in the seventeenth century, and was known as black vomit. It then created the first emergency faced by the newly established United States. In 1793, the disease killed thousands in Philadelphia, the nation's capital at the time. Even President George Washington had to flee the city.

Did you know?

• The Panama Canal took many years to dig between 1880 and 1914, and 25,000 workers died in the process—a lot of them from yellow fever.

• It is illegal to visit several Asian countries without being vaccinated for yellow fever. This is to ensure you cannot introduce it to that country.

GLOSSARY

ABDOMEN
The rear section of an insect, spider or another creepy crawly. The abdomen is sometimes called the tail, but it is much more than that. The abdomen contains most of the animal's intestines and other organs.

ACID
A chemical that attacks other substances, causing burns and other damage. For example, acid makes the skin sore and eats away at metals. Natural acids include lemon juice and fizzy water. Some animals squirt acids at attackers to scare them away.

ALGAE
A living thing that survives in water in the same way as a plant lives on land. They do not eat but convert the energy in sunlight into food. Algae are often tiny things that can only be seen with a microscope, but they sometimes grow in large slimy mats or form into wavy seaweeds.

ANTENNA
The "feeler" on the head of a minibeast. Some are used to feel the way in dark conditions, but they are normally more sensitive to smells and tastes.

BACTERIA
Tiny living things that have a body made of just one cell. Bacteria live everywhere, from the air around us to rocks deep underground. Most bacteria have no effect on humans, although a few can make us ill.

DIGESTION
The process that breaks food apart into simple substances that can be taken into the body and used as fuel or to build up the body. Animals digest their food using several chemicals in their stomachs and intestines.

GRUB
The young form of a beetle. A grub looks like a fat caterpillar, but they are less easy to see. Most live under the ground or hidden inside wood.

HALTERE
A balance system used by flies. A fly's back wings have reduced to small club-shaped stalks that wobble up and down and side to side as the fly swoops and swerves through the air. The movements of the halteres are used by the fly to check the position of its body, working the same kind of way as navigation systems in a airplane cockpit.

INTESTINE
The long tubes that connect the stomach to an animal's bottom. The intestine is where the useful things in food are taken into the body, while the useless waste is prepared to be pushed out of the body.

LARVA
A young version of an insect, that looks and lives in a very different way to the adults. Beetle grubs, caterpillars and maggots are types of larvae. When they have finished growing, the larvae changes completely, becoming the adult form.

MOLLUSC
A large group of animals that includes snails, slugs, shellfish, such as oysters and scallops, as well as squids and octopuses.

NYMPH
A young form of an insect that looks and lives in the same way as the adult – although the nymph will not have any wings in the first part of its life. The nymph develops in several small phases, gradually changing into the adult.

OVIPOSITOR
The tube on the end of a female insect's abdomen that lays eggs. In some cases – especially ants, bees and wasps – the ovipositor has become a stinger that pumps out venom, not eggs.

PARASITE
An animal that survives by living on or inside another animal, known as the host. The host is not usually killed by the parasite, but they may suffer from an illness because of it.

PHEROMONE
A chemical scent released by animals to communicate with each other. The smell of a pheromone is usually used to attract a mate, but in places where many insects are living together in a society, pheromones are used by one "queen" insect to control the lives of the others.

PREY
An animal that is killed and eaten by a hunting animal, or predator.

PROTEIN
A type of chemical that is used to make muscles, skin, hair and many other things inside the body. Proteins are chains of smaller chemicals called amino acids. Each type of protein has a certain order of amino acids in its chain.

SALIVA
The liquid produced in the mouth of an animal. Saliva makes it easier to swallow bits of food, and chemicals in it help with digestion. However, many biting insects use their saliva numb the bite site, stop blood from forming into scabs, and venom is a poisonous type of spit.

SETAE
A hair-like structure covering the bodies of minibeasts which work like sensitive whiskers.

VENOM
A poison produced by an animal that is pumped into a victim. The venom may be used to kill prey or to fend off attackers.

VERTEBRATES
Animals with bones on the inside of the body, especially a backbone or spine.

VIRUS
A tiny disease-causing agent that is half dead and half alive. A virus does not eat or grow in any way like a living thing does. However, the virus does reproduce: It invades a body and uses it to build many more copies of the virus, making the body sick in the process.

INDEX

A–C

ants (*Formica sp*) — 7, 64–5
  antennae — 64
  mouthparts — 64
  waist — 64
aphids (*Aphidoidea*) — 66–7
  rostrum — 66
  too busy for defense — 67
  wax tube — 66
assassin bugs (*Triatominae*) — 164–5
  kissing bugs — 165

bedbugs (*Cimicidae*) — 10–11
  antennae — 10
  sucking tube — 10
bees — 78–9
beetles — 12–13, 42–3, 52–3, 60–1, 90–1, 150–1, 170–1
biting midges (*Ceratopogonidae*) — 114–15
  muffleheads — 115
  nippers — 114
blackflies (*Simulium*) — 166–7
  antennae — 166
  humpback — 167
blowfly (*Calliphora vicina*) — 44
  antennae — 44
  skin case — 44
brine shrimp (*Artemia salina*) — 140–1
  feet — 140
  legs — 140
  sea monkeys — 141
bristleworms (*Amphinomidae*) — 142–3
  body segments — 142
  parapodia — 142
  poisonous bristles — 142
brittle star (*Ophiocoma wendtii*) — 144–5
  color changes — 144
  legs — 144
  starfish — 145
butterflies (*Lepidoptera*) — 68–9
  butterflies and moths — 69
  coiled-up proboscis — 68

caddisflies (*Oxyethira sp*) — 146–7
  angling bait — 147
  breathing pore — 146
  cone — 146
carpet beetles (*Dermestidae*) — 12–13
  antennae — 12
  diet — 13
  head — 12
centipedes (*Lithobius*) — 70–1
  claws — 70
  coordinating the legs — 71
  feeling the way — 70
  legs — 70
cheese mite (*Tyrophagus casei*) — 46–7
  air travel — 46
  burrowers — 46
  making cheese — 47
cicadas (*Cicadoidea*) — 63, 72–3
  paralyzed by wasps — 73
  tymbals — 72
  wings — 72
clothes moth (*Tineola bisselliella*) — 14–15
  antennae — 14
  mouth — 14
  protect your wardrobe — 15
  wings — 14
cockroach (*Periplaneta americana*) — 16–17
  antennae — 16
  claws — 16
  mouth — 16
  neck shield — 16
Colorado Potato Beetle (*Leptinotarsa decemlineata*) — 42–3
  eating machine — 42
  hump back — 42
  spots — 42
cone shells (*Conus sp*) — 168–9
crane flies (*Tipulidae*) — 18–19
  leatherjackets — 19
  legs — 18
  mouth — 18
  thorax — 18

D–G

daddy long-legs spiders (*Pholcidae*) — 20–1
  abdomen — 20
  defense display — 21
  fangs — 20
dangerous species — 163
diving beetles — 139, 150–1
dragonflies (*Odonata*) — 148–9
  large as birds — 149
  water fleas — 148
dung fly (*Scatophaga stercoraria*) — 74–5
  mouth — 74
  robber flies — 75
  sensory hairs — 74
dust mite (*Dermatophagoides pteronyssinus*) — 22–3
  invisible mites — 23
  mouth — 22
  setae (hairs) — 22

earthworm (*Lumbricus terrestris*) — 76–7
  body segments — 76
  hooked hairs — 76
  worm charmers — 77
earwigs (*Dermaptera*) — 24–5
  abdomen — 24
  caring parents — 25
  cerci — 24
  wing cases — 24
eyelash mite (*Demodex folliculorum*) — 116–17
  allergies — 117
  heads — 116
  legs — 116
  size — 116

fire-detecting beetle (*Melanophila acuminata*) — 170–1
fleas — 122–3, 128–9
fruit fly (*Drosophila melanogaster*) — 48–9
  antennae — 48
  scientific research — 49
  sucking tube — 48
  wings — 48

grain weevil (*Sitophilus granarius*) — 50–1
  antennae — 50
  cereal destroyer — 51
  face — 50
  wing cases — 50
great diving beetle (*Dytiscus marginalis*) — 150–1
  back — 150
  biters — 150
  light seekers — 151
  paddles — 150

H–J

ham beetle (*Necrobia ruficollis*) — 52–3
  antennae — 52
  Egyptian mummies — 53
  hairy back — 52
  mouth — 52
head louse (*Pediculus humanus*) — 118–19
  body — 118
  feet — 118
  nits — 118
Hobo Spider — 29
honeybee (*Apis mellifera*) — 78–9
  manufacturing honey — 79
  taste testers — 78
hookworm (*Ancylostoma duodenale*) — 120–1
  allergies — 121
  head — 120
  roundworm — 120
hornet (*Vespa crabro*) — 80–1
  deadly hornets — 81
  mouth — 80
  wings — 80
house spider (*Tegenaria domestica*) — 28–9
  pedipalps — 28
housefly (*Musca domestica*) — 26–7
  halter — 26
  kaleidoscope vision — 27
  wings — 26
hover flies (*Syrphidae*) — 82–3
  antennae — 82
  flower food — 82

rat-tailed maggots 83
human flea (*Pulex irritans*) 122–3
  Black Death 122
  jumping 122
  mouth 122
  wingless 122

jellyfish (*Scyphozoa*) 152–3
  body opening 152
  self-illumination 153
  skin 152
  stingers 152
jumping spiders (*Salticidae*) 84–5
  fangs 84
  mating display 85
  palps 84

L–M

lacewing (*Chrysoperla carnea*) 86–7
  mating signals 87
  pincer movement 86
  waste management 86
  wings 86
ladybug (*Coccinella septempunctata*) 88–9
  bloody message 88
  false eyes 88
  hard cover 88
  religious connection 89
leech (*Hirudo medicinalis*) 124–5
  body breather 124
  mouth 124
  sucker 124
lice 118–19
liver fluke (*Fasciola hepatica*) 126–7
  body 126
  mating 127
  mouth 126
locusts (*Orthoptera*) 172–3
long horned beetles (*Cerambycidae*) 90–1
  antennae 90
  fur coat 90
  twig girdlers 91
Lyme disease tick (*Ixodes ricinus*) 174–5

maggots 9, 54–5
  cleaning wounds 55
  leatherjackets 19
  mouthparts 54

rat-tailed maggots 83
  worm-shaped 54
malaria mosquito (*Anopheles sp*) 176–7
  Africa 177
  antennae 176
  blood straw 176
mange mites (*Sarcoptidae*) 30–1
  domed body 30
  feet 30
  mating 30
meal moth (*Plodia interpunctella*) 56–7
  antennae 56
  light seeker 56
  trapping moths 57
mealybugs (*Planococcus sp*) 58–9
  ants and mealybugs 59
  feeding spike 58
midges 7, 114–15
millipedes (*Diplopoda*) 92–3
  legs 92
  senses 92
  shedding skin 93
mites 7, 22–3, 30–1, 46–7, 108–9, 113, 116–17, 130–1
mosquitoes 176–7, 184–5, 188–9
moths 14–15, 56–7, 69

P–S

paper wasps (*Polistes sp*) 94–5
  cell nursery 94
  feeding time 94
  nest defense 95
  paper walls 94
paralysis tick (*Rhipicephalus sanguineus*) 178–9
parasitic wasps (*Aphidius*) 96–7
  egg tube 96
  searching for grubs 97
pests 41
pond snails (*Lymnaeidae*) 139, 154–5
  breathing 155
  shell 154

ragworm (*Nereis succinca*) 156–7
  color change 156
  Moon 157
  teeth 156
robber flies 75
rosemary beetle (*Chrysolina americana*) 60–1

metallic stripes 60
  wings 60

sand flea (*Tunga penetrans*) 128–9
  black spot 128
  chiggers 129
  legs 128
  skin 128
sandflies (*Phlebotomos sp*) 180–1
scabies mites (*Sarcoptes sp*) 130–1
  blind 130
  diagnosis 131
  nymph 130
scale insects (*Coccoidea*) 98–9
  antennae 98
  cochineal insects 99
  waxed back 98
sea urchins (*Echinoidea*) 158–9
  cone shape 158
  stomach 158, 159
  tentacles 158
silverfish (*Thysanura*) 32–3
  antennae 32
  bristletails 32
  nymphs 33
slugs (*Gastropoda*) 100–1
  hidden shell 100
  slug slime 101
  tentacle 100
spiders 9, 20–1, 28–9, 34–5, 84–5
  web 34–5
  web silk 35
springtails (*Collembola*) 102–3
  hexapods 102
  mouth 102
  tail 102
stable fly (*Stomoxys calcitrans*) 132–3
  egg tube 132
  sucker 132
stinkbug (*Palomena prasina*) 104–5
  digesting food 104
  shield 104
  squirt 104
  tube feeder 104

T–Y

tapeworm (*Taenia pisiformis*) 134–5
  head 134

hooks 134
  lions 135
tarantulas (*Theraphosidae*) 182–3
termites 36–7
threadworm (*Trichostrongylus vitrinus*) 136–7
  infection 137
  tail 136
thrips (*Thysanoptera*) 106–7
  baby thrips 107
  juice probe 106
  wings 106
ticks 174–5, 178–9
tiger mosquito (*Aedes albopictus*) 184–5
tsetse fly (*Glossina sp*) 186–7
  blood tube 186
  feeding bulb 186
  wings 186

velvet mites (*Trombidiidae*) 108–9
  fangs 108
  hairs 108

wasps 63, 94–5, 96–7
water bears (*Echiniscus sp*) 160–1
  body 160
  claws 160
  survivors 161
wood termite (*Coptotermes niger*) 36–7
  feelers 36
  mouthparts 36
  termites and ants 37
woodlouse (*Armadillidium sp*) 110–11
  eyes 110
  flexible plates 110
  sea creatures 111
  skin 110
woodworm (*Anobium punctatum*) 38
  head 30
  slow-grower 31
worms 113
  earthworm 76–7
  leech 124–5
  marine worms 139, 142–3, 156–7
  parasitic worms 120–1, 126–7, 134–5, 136–7

yellow-fever mosquito (*Aedes aegypti*) 188–9
  antennae 188
  disease 189